"A unique and fascinating peek behind the scenes of this blossoming branch of coaching, *Inside Creativity Coaching* will prove an inspiring resource for creatives and coaches alike."
　　　—Eva Weaver, creativity coach and author, *The Puppet Boy of Warsaw*

"Creative and performing artists will get as much out of *Inside Creativity Coaching* as coaches and therapists will. These forty case studies present a clear picture of the challenges that creatives face—and what they can do to meet those challenges. Highly recommended!"
　　　—Roccie Hill, Executive Director, Mendocino Art Center

Inside Creativity Coaching

In *Inside Creativity Coaching*, 40 creativity coaches from around the world describe their work with creative clients in this first-ever case study examination of the art and practice of creativity coaching.

Curated by one of America's foremost creativity coaches, these rich narratives examine how creativity coaches work with writers, painters, musicians, craftspeople, and other creatives on issues such as motivation, procrastination, blockage, and performance and career anxiety. Packed with concrete tools and techniques, the book draws on inspirational success stories from across the globe to help coaches better understand and serve their creative clients. It will be a valuable resource for creativity coaches, coaches interested in developing a specialty, and creatives and performing artists looking to overcome their challenges.

Covering a diverse range of disciplines, *Inside Creativity Coaching* is a must-have book for both aspiring and experienced creativity coaches, and anyone interested in helping creatives.

Eric Maisel, PhD, is a retired family therapist, active creativity coach, and the author of more than 50 books, including *Coaching the Artist Within* and *Secrets of a Creativity Coach*. He writes the "Rethinking Mental Health" blog for *Psychology Today* and leads workshops and lectures worldwide.

Inside Creativity Coaching

40 Inspiring Case Studies from Around the World

EDITED BY ERIC MAISEL

Routledge
Taylor & Francis Group

NEW YORK AND LONDON

First published 2020
by Routledge
52 Vanderbilt Avenue, New York, NY 10017

and by Routledge
2 Park Square, Milton Park, Abingdon, Oxon, OX14 4RN

Routledge is an imprint of the Taylor & Francis Group, an informa business

© 2020 Eric Maisel

Library of Congress Cataloging-in-Publication Data
Names: Maisel, Eric, 1947- editor.
Title: Inside creativity coaching : 40 inspiring case studies from around the
    world / edited by Eric Maisel.
Description: New York, NY : Routledge, 2020. | Includes bibliographical
    references and index.
Identifiers: LCCN 2019018427 (print) | LCCN 2019019299 (ebook) |
    ISBN 9780429269172 (ebook) | ISBN 9780367219826 (hardback : alk.
    paper) | ISBN 9780367219833 (pbk. : alk. paper)
Subjects: LCSH: Creative ability—Case studies. | Creation (Literary,
    artistic, etc.)—Case studies. | Personal coaching—Case studies.
Classification: LCC BF408 (ebook) | LCC BF408 .I547 2020 (print) |
    DDC 153.3/5—dc23
LC record available at https://lccn.loc.gov/2019018427

ISBN: 978-0-367-21982-6 (hbk)
ISBN: 978-0-367-21983-3 (pbk)
ISBN: 978-0-429-26917-2 (ebk)

Typeset in Avenir and Dante
by Apex CoVantage, LLC

Contents

Introduction   *xiii*

1. **Risk and Detachment: The Keys to a Successful Design
   Career**   **1**
   Ariel Grace

2. **The Timid Creative: How a Writer Found Her Resolve**   **6**
   Clare Thorbes

3. **The Unauthorized Artist: Coaching a Self-Taught Painter**   **11**
   Elise V. Allan

4. **A Meaningful Writing Career: How Values and Creative
   Work Can Align**   **16**
   Gina Edwards

5. **A Musician's 'Impossible Dream': Overcoming Stage
   Fright With Creativity Coaching**   **21**
   Nick Lazaris

6. **Della's Dream Comes True: Subpersonality Work With a
   Blocked Writer**   **26**
   Marj Penley

7. **A Change of Scenery May Be Just the Ticket: How
   Creativity and Travel Can Help Reinvent Midlife**   **31**
   Jan Moore

8. **An Artist Prepares: How Dreams Can Come True Sooner
   Than You Expect**   36
   Sharon Good

9. **Start Where You Are: How a Blocked Creativity Coach
   Finally Wrote Her Case Study**   41
   Rachel Marsden

10. **A Filmmaker Returns to Health: Creativity Coaching for
    Overall Wellbeing**   46
    Nefeli Soteriou

11. **Out of the Woods: A Talented Artist Returns to the
    Marketplace**   51
    Sheryl Garratt

12. **How Samson Grew His Hair Back: A Photographer Prevails**   56
    Rahti Gorfien

13. **When Pain Strikes: Building a New Life After a Divorce**   61
    Rosa Phoenix

14. **Foiling Perfectionism: The Magic of Lowered Expectations** 66
    Jill Badonsky

15. **How Confidence Breeds Creativity: A Retired Reporter
    Breaks Free From Self-Doubt**   71
    Halli Bourne

16. **The Ugly Sculpture That Wasn't: Jennifer Rediscovers Her
    Creative Identity**   76
    Sharon J. Burton

17. **Small, Simple, and Every Day: Constructing a Creative Life** 81
    Stephanie Christie

18. **A Writer in Search of a Practice: How Coaching Launched
    a Hundred Consecutive Days of Writing**   86
    Jude Walsh

19. **We're All in This Together: How Group Creativity Coaching Provides Support**   **90**
Doreen Marcial Poreba

20. **A Whirlwind Trapped in a Coffee Cup: Fearing Art-Making When Art Is Linked to Suffering**   **95**
Beatriz Martínez Barrio

21. **A Colorless World: How Creativity Coaching Restored Vibrancy to One Painter's Life**   **100**
Natalie Dadamio

22. **Art as Money: Creating for Yourself and Not Just for Success**   **105**
Steph Cohen

23. **Helping a Designer Grow Her Confidence: Steps to a Design Career**   **110**
Sally Mazák

24. **Phyllis Draws a Postcard: Time-Limited Creative Exercises in Session**   **115**
Nancy Johnston

25. **Using the Enneagram in Creativity Coaching: An Example at Point Nine**   **119**
Janet Johnston

26. **How Lynn Got Her Sew-Jo Back: Clearing Physical and Mental Clutter to Unleash Creativity**   **123**
Nadia Arbach

27. **The Coaching Side to Private Tutoring: Preparing the Ground for a Successful Outcome**   **129**
Susanne Rieger

28. **The Guitar or the Code: From Tech Day Job to Full-Time Musician**   **133**
Pragati Chaudhry

29. **Alison the Ambitious Academic: Managing Overwhelm and Inefficiency Caused by Competing Demands**   137
Vinita Joseph

30. **Alex Markets Himself as An Artist: An Artist Learns to Believe in Himself and His Art**   141
Niki Anandi Koulouri

31. **"I'm Just Not Good Enough": How to Stop the Naysaying and Fulfill Your Creative Potential**   146
Angela Terris

32. **Burning Down the House: One Writer Rewrites Her Book From Scratch**   151
April Bosshard

33. **Wooing the Muse With Wellness: How a Foundation of Health and Well-Being Can Spark New Creative Energy**   156
Danielle Raine

34. **Working With What Is: Committing to Creative Work While Facing Obligations**   161
Regina de Búrca

35. **Refilling the Creative Well: Finding Voice and Flow Through Writing and Journaling**   166
Jackee Holder

36. **Orange Disks and Orange Balls: How a Visual Storyteller Stopped Self-Sabotaging**   171
Francesca Aniballi

37. **Bumping Into Walls: Navigating the Maze of Creativity**   176
Lori Barraco Sylvester

38. **The Cracks in the Pavement: Liminal Spaces and Creativity**   181
Litza Bixler

39. **A Leadership Journey to Purpose: Personal Breakthroughs From Leading Others**   186
Tania Kelvin

40. **The Magic of an Escape, a Goal, and a Deadline:**
A Playwright Finishes Her Musical and Writes a Play
in a Week   **190**
Jenny Maguire

Appendix: Tips for Creativity Coaches and Prospective Coaches   *196*
Appendix: Supplemental Reading   *215*
Index   *217*

Introduction

My name is Eric Maisel, and I'm a creativity coach. I've been doing this work for more than 30 years now. First, I was a novelist; then I became a psychotherapist (technically, a licensed marriage and family therapist); then I glided into creativity coaching, inventing the territory as I went.

This is a typical route for creativity coaches: to have a background in the arts and a second background as a therapist or helping professional of some sort and to parlay that experience and those interests into a niche career that they themselves design. Nobody comes out of college a creativity coach. We are all born along the way, often in our mid to late 30s or later.

I've also been writing for 50 years. Over the course of those many years, I've written 50 or more books. This, too, is quite typical: creativity coaches are usually creators who, sometimes maybe only in fits and starts, keep at their art while they coach. It is the rare creativity coach who doesn't have an art discipline he or she loves and works at some of the time. The majority of creativity coaches are writers (novelists, poets, nonfiction writers, screenwriters), and the next largest group is made up of visual artists (with many craftspeople included), but every artistic and intellectual discipline is represented, including the hard sciences.

As a creativity coach, I work with world-famous creators and unknown creators. I work with regularly producing creators, blocked creators, and would-be creators. Some of my clients have bestsellers to their credit, million-selling albums, hit television shows, and a net worth of eight or nine figures. Most have day jobs and trouble making ends meet. All share a certain set of attributes and beliefs about the world. They feel fulfilled, if only for a moment, when they create well. Creating is how they make their meaning.

They are challenged by their own personality, by the work of creating, and by their culture and society. And they can all use the guidance and support that creativity coaches provide.

I've been working as a creativity coach for a long time. I began calling myself a creativity coach 30 years ago, perhaps coining the term in the process. Indeed, this field is very new. Most creativity coaches only began coaching in the past 15 years. Many of these new creativity coaches have only the smallest of practices. Because the field of creativity coaching is very new, few creative people know anything about creativity coaching, even that it exists. Hopefully, this book will change that a bit.

I think this will indeed change as more people enter this embryonic field and call themselves creativity coaches. I am helping some number of people do just that. In addition to working with clients—by phone, by Skype, by email, in groups and in workshops—I also train creativity coaches. Coaches-in-training and the clients they coach during trainings live in Paris, Singapore, New Zealand, Switzerland, Germany, the rural South, Los Angeles, everywhere and anywhere that email, phone, and Skype can reach.

What do creativity coaches do? They help clients create and make meaning. With their clients, they investigate issues of blockage, self-doubt, anxiety, fear of failure, worries about mistakes, and the other process and personality issues that interfere with getting creative work done. They help creators deal with marketplace issues, career issues, issues of isolation and alienation, and the other issues that inevitably arise for people who have chosen to create. They cheerlead, listen, educate, respond, and help their creative clients get their work done while living in the real world.

In the process, creativity coaches also become much more effective self-coaches. The creativity coaches I train find it impossible not to look at their own creativity issues as they work with clients and think long and hard about what helps and hinders creative expression. A coach-in-training begins to see why she never finished her mystery novel as she works with a blocked painter or a blocked composer. Another coach-in-training discovers that her negative self-talk has caused her to stand on the creativity sidelines. Coaches-in-training learn that they can be of great help to their clients; they also learn how to help themselves.

Never before has it been possible for two people separated by great distances to communicate with each other so quickly, easily, and cheaply. A creativity coach in Ireland can work with a client in Israel, and a writer in Georgia and a painter in Delhi can work with the same creativity coach in Chicago. One of the many advantages of this new reality is that coaches, who could not possibly build a practice in their locale because it isn't home to enough creative people, can begin to build a real practice by reaching out across the country and around the world.

Creativity coaching can mean various things. In the world of business, for example, it tends to mean the art of helping individuals, groups, and organizations become better problem-solvers and innovators. By creativity coaching, I mean something rather different from that. I mean the activity of one person helping another person with every aspect of that person's creative life, including the psychological, emotional, existential, and practical problems that arise as the client tries to create. Virtually nothing is out of bounds as a creativity coach endeavors to help his client write, paint, invent, or compose, find and make meaning, maintain emotional health, enjoy a measure of happiness, and lead a good life in which creating is a centerpiece activity.

Probably this could also be called life coaching for creative people. A creative in need of a creativity coach is not looking for a psychotherapist, a marketing guru, a painting class, or a class in creativity. Instead, she is looking for the kind of support and direction that is not offered in art schools, counseling clinics, pastoral offices, or career centers. She is one of the countless people who feel an inner necessity to manifest potential and make meaning but who come up against inner and outer obstacles and become blocked and thwarted. She needs someone who can help with that.

In my own case, I am trained as a psychotherapist, and that informs what I do; and I have been a writer for 50 years, which also informs what I do. But creativity coaching is not psychotherapy, and it is not the teaching of writing, painting, inventing, composing, acting, and so on. Rather, creativity coaching encompasses the whole of a client's life and the totality of human nature in a way that not even pastoral counseling or psychotherapy does. A cleric may invite you to do soul work. A psychotherapist may invite you to do personality work. But a creativity coach invites you to think hard, feel deeply, dream big, and be great. A creativity coach invites you to manifest your potential. A creativity coach asks you to step up to the plate and live a vital, authentic life.

Because that is a lot to ask and because almost all people are burdened in ways that make it hard for them to create, I have to be modest about what I expect from my clients. At the same time, because clients know that not creating is the equivalent of spiritual or existential death, they will only respond if a lot is asked of them. So, I have to hold out a large vision. This is the path a creativity coach walks, setting out the baby steps that a client is able to take while at the same time honoring the client's need to do work that is deep and grand. The client may hunger to be a new Shakespeare or Mozart but may only get a few indifferent lines or lyrics penned this month. That is not enough but it is also not to be sneered at. A creativity coach builds on that modest but real success to urge clients on further.

What ought a creativity coach know and understand? She ought to know and understand the following six things: (1) the creative process, (2) the creative personality, (3) existential reality, (4) practical reality, (5) human nature, and (6) how to help. That's all, really. She only needs to know just about everything. Of course, we will all fall short of this ideal. But there really is an ideal, and our goal is to approach these lofty heights.

For this book, I invited creativity coaches from around the world to supply me with an example of their work with a single client (or, in some cases, a single class or support group). Many of these case studies show only the most modest results. That's as it is. If a client who has not written for years begins to write for 15 minutes a week, that is not particularly 'earth shaking' or 'life transforming.' Or is it? By the way, because these case studies come from around the world, the first language of a coach may be Greek, German, Spanish, Italian, or some other language that is not English. I wanted something of that flavor to remain, and it has.

Two other notes. First, care has been taken to maintain the anonymity of case study subjects, either by minimizing or altering details or by creating composites. Second, in addition to the case study proper, contributors have also included learning points and self-coaching questions. The learning points nicely summarize the main points of the case study. With regard to the self-coaching questions, if you're a creative, they will help you meet the process, personality, and career challenges that you face. If you're a coach, you can profitably use the self-coaching questions in your work with your creative clients.

I hope that you enjoy the 40 case studies included in this book. I think they provide an interesting picture of who creativity coaches are, what issues their clients present, and how they work to help clients achieve their goals. If you've been thinking about becoming a coach, these case studies may perhaps help you make up your mind. If you're a coach or therapist looking to add creativity coaching to your repertoire, I hope that this collection inspires you to do just that. And if you're a creative person, I hope that you see in these case studies the glimmer of answers to the challenges that you face. Please enjoy!

Risk and Detachment 1

The Keys to a Successful Design Career

Ariel Grace

"I doubt they'll let me try again," Taylor lamented in despair, trying to hold his voice steady. I could tell that his heart was tightening as his voice quieted. We were speaking on the phone, but I sensed he was swallowing tears, trying to remain strong.

He explained how frustrated he was: "I worked so hard, I stayed up all night, and they totally tore my work to pieces." I sensed a hint of self-righteousness hiding behind his feelings of not having been appreciated. He wanted to lash out, to blame the people he was working with for being so heartless and cruel. His career dreams were being crushed inside of a chaotic deadline that was overextending him on multiple levels. Or, at least, that was the story he was telling me.

Just a few weeks before, we had worked together to discover his true dream of moving from a research profession to a user experience designer. He was so excited. In working together, he disclosed that he was fearful because he didn't know if his skill set would be "good enough" to be recognized as a designer. He didn't trust that people would take him seriously because he hadn't built strong skills in that area. He felt that he couldn't completely start over in his career because he needed to make a living. I encouraged him to find opportunities at his present job, even if it meant taking some risks. Everything seemed to be heading in a positive direction.

Taylor began to look for any opportunity he could find to take on design work. However, in his enthusiasm to do a great job and move forward with his dreams, he quickly overcommitted and overextended himself. He was determined to prove that he could excel. He volunteered to lead a design effort in a high-risk, poorly managed project. The intentions were good with everyone involved, but the experience quickly went south.

Taylor worked day and night trying to "get it right" and produce something that would work for the required design needs. He spent hours by himself creating the "perfect" designs before he showed them to stakeholders. He knew they were going to love it. They were rapidly approaching their deadline for development, and the stakeholders were getting impatient. When he reviewed it with them; they were very unhappy with the designs and highly critical about the direction he had gone.

Not only that but now they were potentially going to have to go to development without design input because of the deadline being so close. The call ended with Taylor feeling ashamed and disheartened. He was unaccustomed to receiving criticism for his work. It felt very uncomfortable, and he quickly got defensive. In the end, he had to scrap everything, which felt like a personal affront to his efforts and creative expression. Taylor was devastated, not only because he had tried so hard to perform but also because he was losing his hope about his future in design.

As we unpacked what had happened, Taylor and I realized there were several breakdowns in expectations and communication that had occurred during the frenzy to get the work completed. To start, Taylor had not explained his level of expertise when he volunteered to do the work because he was fearful of the potential rejection of not being able to take on the project. Not sharing his truth and his vulnerability created a situation in which the expectations of his level of skills were distorted.

After some scenario dialogue work together, Taylor realized that he should have been clearer and set stronger boundaries about what type of design work he could truly support. Also, when Taylor received such strong criticism, he felt defensive. This can be a natural response when someone is used to being a top performer and is unaccustomed to not hitting the mark. He wanted to blame someone. That is what anger creates—a desire to lash outward or protect one's self from further injury.

He got frustrated with himself instead of continuing to have conversations with the stakeholders. He directed his anger inward and created even more angst. We discussed the idea of "failing fast" and that there really are no mistakes in life. Eventually, he was able to create some self-compassion for what had happened. Together we designed a meditation and breath work practice for Taylor. This helped him to be able to work with his discomfort when something came up that made him feel "wrong," "not good enough" or like a "failure."

After realizing that what he felt was a "failure" was actually a series of misunderstandings and unclear boundaries, Taylor was able to shift his perspective about what had happened and forgive himself for rushing to conclusions. From this place, he realized that the criticism he received was not actually as aggressive as he had originally thought. Rather, he was feeling defensive and angry in the moment. Taylor was able to go back to the stakeholders and explain what had happened from a place of humility, respect, and care. He apologized for not being clear, explained that he had the best of intentions, and made amends with the team. It felt really uncomfortable to have the conversation; in the end, however, the team's relationships actually improved through honest conversation about the situation.

In coaching Taylor, I helped him to develop an ability to create personal detachment from his artistic expression in a work context where form and customer fit are often more important than personal expression. So often creatives get this confused and bring their passion for pure expression of art to scenarios that do not require it. Moving through discomfort and growing as a designer allowed the opportunity to discuss options for more shared design and better outcomes for the customers.

Essentially, through his "failure," Taylor realized he was maturing and growing, not only into a better designer but also into a stronger leader and group facilitator. To meet his creative expression needs outside of work, he began to play the guitar again and channel some of his artistic expression into writing songs.

As we continued to work together, Taylor realized he needed a more "safe" and low-pressure opportunity to learn and to grow his portfolio. We discussed the concept of "disposable designs," iterations, and testing his work with multiple customers, before showing it to stakeholders. This maturity curve is often something that happens with people who desire to creatively express and to turn that product into a business. It takes time to figure out how to marry form and function with customer needs.

I encouraged him to create small, real-world examples outside of work, with low-fidelity, sketchy designs, and test them with people. Taylor began to feel more comfortable in his ability to convey creative ideas and move into his next steps of becoming a user experience (UX) designer. He then signed up for taking courses in digital design and began to feel more confident that he would be able to find work in this field.

As we continued to work together, Taylor began to feel more comfortable in adopting this new identity. He began to talk about his new way of working in casual conversion more often, creating new and unexpected opportunities for him to try out his skills. Eventually, Taylor made the transition to being a true UX designer, blending his research skills and his love for design into a multi-passionate career and growing as a person along the way.

As it turned out, what seemed at first like a "trial by fire," high-pressure experience turned into one of the largest growth and learning opportunities of Taylor's life. He was able to become a better communicator, set clear boundaries with his time and effort, and create more balance in his creative expression. He no longer worked until the wee hours because he no longer felt like he needed to prove himself to anyone.

His experience of his own intrinsic worth became less attached to his way of working. His skills became more deeply rooted in his ability to navigate his life experiences with honesty and self-trust. It took a while to grow into the creative job that he wanted, but eventually, Taylor realized it was never really about the job and always about the person he wanted to become.

Learning Points

1. Take steps toward your creative expression for work or play that feel safe and low risk when you are getting started. Size is up to you, and what matters are how much it makes you feel uncomfortable and how much discomfort you are willing to work through.
2. If you are trying to pivot your career into a creative position that requires a lot of new skills, consider what type of courses, learnings, and real-world opportunities you need that will support your growth.
3. If you can begin to "feel and act" like the person you are wanting to become and speak about your desires in casual conversation, over time you will feel more comfortable actualizing into that person and obtaining the skills you need.

Self-Coaching Questions

1. Is there a skill set or creative outlet that you have not let yourself try but that you keep secretly wanting to express? Are there particular things that "keep coming back" even when you push them aside? What might happen if you began? What fear is stopping you?

2. Have you blocked yourself from beginning because something has to happen first? (An example would be, "I will start a band when I find a guitarist.") Jot down some of the "lies we tell ourselves" about why you cannot create in a certain way.

3. Have you set yourself back in your creative endeavors because you received criticism? Have you pushed yourself too far beyond your comfort zone and then shut down? What would it take to reopen to your desire?

About Ariel Grace

Ariel Grace helps closeted and blocked creatives and soulpreneurs become wildly successful and well paid and birth their soul's gifts into the world. She has led creative teams for more than a decade and deeply understands the tension between art and service. She believes that what is missing most from our world are soulful connection and playful, creative ways of being. There is always a way for the burnt-out creative to design a next level life. Check out Ariel's latest offerings at https://linktr.ee/arielgracefull.

The Timid Creative　　　**2**

How a Writer Found Her Resolve

Clare Thorbes

Julia approached me because she wanted to write a children's book but couldn't seem to get anywhere with it. She was unsure of her writer's identity and doubted her ability to pull off the project. She wondered whether the whole idea was too silly because her mind seemed to be taking her in all sorts of fanciful directions.

During our first phone call, I asked whether she had ever submitted anything to a publisher. She said that she had. Her first story had been rejected, and though she tried again, she received another rejection letter.

"Congratulations," I said. "Many writers never get past the first rejection. Do you think rejection is a normal part of the writing life?"

"I'm not sure. I imagine someone with real talent would get accepted."

"Would you like to research published authors who faced rejection early in their careers?"

"Yes, that might help."

Julia learned that many of her favorite authors had experienced a string of rejections. Some ended up self-publishing but attracted the interest of mainstream publishers after their story proved popular with readers.

"What struck me was the various ways these writers dealt with rejection. In some cases, they didn't take it personally at all."

"It's great that you noticed that, Julia. We do have a choice in how we react. One author I know got a rejection letter that ended with, 'Sincerely sorry to have read this manuscript.'"

Julia laughed and said, "Maybe I could develop a rejection benchmark. If it isn't cleverly written, I won't let it penetrate, and if it is, appreciating the wit will take some of the sting out of it."

We talked about other rituals Julia could develop around rejection that would acknowledge the wound but allow her to carry on. Julia hadn't heard of Ellen Langer, the author of *On Becoming an Artist*, and I quoted a passage to her, "Evaluations are made by people based on their experience and their own needs. They are not handed down from the heavens . . . if we don't take the compliment, we're not vulnerable to the insult."

When we spoke again, Julia said she had managed several pages of writing that week. "I really only have to please myself. Of course, that's another issue."

"Hmm, sounds like some inner critic involvement. Can you tell me what's been happening with that?" I asked.

"Well, I'm questioning every plot and character choice. I'll write for a bit; then after I read it, I tear it up in disgust. I keep thinking it's so implausible, but these silly ideas just keep coming. It's been like this for years."

"What would happen if you wrote until you're spent for that session and then put the writing away without looking at it?"

"I guess I could try that and see whether it makes a difference."

Julia reported that she had written almost every day the previous week and had yet to look back at the results. "It was quite freeing, knowing that I had postponed judging the work."

"Yes, it's like trying to wear two different hats at the same time, isn't it?" I left her with the question, "How else could you manage your inner critic because you'll eventually have to look at your work and revise it?"

A week later, Julia said, "I told my critic, quite graphically, to leave me alone. But then I realized it's just trying to protect me. So, I decided I would start by looking for the good bits I want to keep instead of immediately hunting for flaws. I actually looked at a whole chapter of writing but with compassion this time—although I didn't ignore the things that needed fixing."

I congratulated her and encouraged her to continue refining her revision process. I suggested we come back to how she was feeling about the content during our next call.

Julia cancelled our next appointment, and when she didn't reschedule, I wondered whether I had been too directive or had triggered her in some way. When I checked in with her by email, Julia said she hadn't written at all in the interim. We scheduled a phone call to explore what might have gotten her off track.

The first thing she said was, "You know, when I saw your ad and decided to email you, I hesitated quite a while before I clicked *Send*. I kept hearing my husband's voice in my head: 'What could a coach possibly do for you? If you really were a writer, you'd be doing it more.'"

"Do you know any writers or other creative people?"

"Not really. Most of our circle consists of my husband's friends. They're all small businesspeople like he is."

"It sounds like he has an informal advisory group. Has he found that helpful?"

"Oh, I know where you're going with this!" Julia interrupted. "I can create something like that for my writing."

The following week Julia confided, "I dreamt about my aunt this week. I lived with her until my late teens after my parents died. I haven't thought about this for years, but I used to write little picture books. You know, just a few pages of text and drawings. One day my aunt, who was quite stern, found my stories and said, 'Why are you wasting time on this rubbish?' She tore up my stories and fed them into the fireplace! I cried for days, but she had no patience with any of it."

"I'm so sorry that happened to you, Julia. Have you spoken with anyone about this period in your life?"

"I've done some counseling about losing my parents and how harsh she was in general but not about this. Do you think that's why I haven't taken myself seriously as a writer?"

"We could try a visioning exercise, if you're game." When Julia expressed interest, I gave her the task of taking some quiet time and imagining what it would feel like to have at least one person in her life who unconditionally supported her writing.

"That was really powerful," Julia reported during our next conversation. "I could imagine what it would be like to have that safety net of support. I know I wouldn't let the least little thing stop me."

"That's wonderful, Julia. You could recall that vision the next time something makes you doubt yourself. Is this a good time to talk about your story? What makes you think it's silly or implausible?"

"Well, the things that come to mind as I'm writing seem so far-fetched! I've never heard of singing trees, for example."

"In that case, I applaud you again for continuing to write, considering your feel this way about the content. Do you think your audience of children would find your story far-fetched? Or are you viewing the story from an adult perspective?"

"You're right. I'm viewing it through the eyes of the least imaginative people I know," Julia replied, laughing.

"What sort of fanciful children's books are on the market these days? There's the unicorn craze, of course, but could you find some other examples?"

"I'm going to head straight to the bookstore after this call," Julia decided.

"The last time we spoke, you mentioned your husband said that you'd be doing more writing if you were a 'real writer.' When you've finished your children's book research, could you spend some time thinking about how you could claim your identity as a writer?"

"Oh, I love the way you put that! My identity as a writer. Thank you; I will think about that."

"Great! I'm curious to hear what you come up with."

I could hear the excitement in Julia's voice when we spoke again. "You'll never believe this! My husband walked by when I was writing this week and said, 'Oh, you're writing, are you?' I screwed up my courage and told him, 'Yes, I am. This is very important to me, and I'm devoting the afternoon to it.' I took a deep breath and then I said, 'And every other afternoon this week, too.'"

"Fabulous, Julia! What did he say?"

"I thought he'd be furious. You could have knocked me over with a feather when he said, 'That's the resolve I've been waiting for. I was going to ask you to help me with the bookkeeping, but it can wait.'"

"I'm really happy for you, Julia."

"Now that I have his support, I'm going to find a writer's group so I can get feedback as the story goes along. I did try a group before, but some of their comments were acidic. One person actually said to someone who outlined their story idea, 'Oh, that'll never work.' I never went back."

"It takes time to find a supportive group. Remember, if it doesn't already exist, you can create a group of your own."

As we wrapped up the call, we agreed that our coaching had come to an end but that I would be available for periodic check-ins and that she could always call on me if new obstacles arose.

Learning Points

1. Internal and external obstacles to creativity aren't always obvious, but they're worth unearthing and examining.
2. It's a good idea to test your assumptions about your genre and your place in it.
3. Emotional self-management is a vital part of your development as a creative person.

Self-Coaching Questions

1. How will you handle audience reaction to your work at all stages of your career?
2. If your loved ones aren't supportive of your creativity, where can you find that support?
3. What ground rules might you establish in a creativity support group?

About Clare Thorbes

Clare Thorbes is a certified creativity coach based in Ottawa, Canada, who works with writers, visual artists, and performers. Her goal is to be her clients' ally as they build a life in the arts. She publishes *Block-Buster*, a creativity newsletter, on her website: www.clarethorbescreativitycoach.com. She is a visual artist (www.clarethorbes.com; www.facebook.com/clarethorbesportraits), a multilingual translator, and an editor who has helped novelists and nonfiction writers across Canada bring their creations to life.

The Unauthorized Artist

3

Coaching a Self-Taught Painter

Elise V. Allan

Gina's first email gave me just the right amount of information but ended with an apology for rambling on too much. A full-time visual artist, largely self-taught, she was showing work in a couple of galleries. "I can see that this is a sign of progress," she wrote, "but I have problems with self-belief and confidence."

Torn between wanting to contribute her share of the family income and a longing to make deeper work that would draw on her inner life, she was scared that the new work she dreamt of doing would be unmarketable, imagining that the galleries would disapprove of it—along with the entire art establishment, potential buyers, and even her husband, who might be left to foot all the bills. We arranged to meet by Zoom for six monthly sessions, emailing between meetings.

In person she was warm and likeable, covering a lot of ground quickly. She spoke enthusiastically about a variety of interesting ideas she wanted to work with and about her fear of letting down her husband and teenage sons. She'd reached burnout in her previous career; she was desperate not to return to it, and this added to the pressure to sell. I could sense her care about her family's needs and her struggle to take care of her own needs and wants. It was also clear that she saw the art world as filled with authority figures and herself as an inferior outsider.

We began by talking about how she might create a space where she could work without feeling someone was looking over her shoulder. Her studio was between a large open-plan kitchen, the hub of the house, and a cloakroom, so her husband and sons regularly walked through and would comment on her work in progress. She realized that she could swap her studio to the spare room at the other end of their apartment, where she was less likely to be interrupted.

We also devised a boundary around her time. She committed to one day a week doing experimental work, free from pressure to sell or to please others, sacred time that ignored business concerns. To avoid comments, she wouldn't show this experimental work to her husband and sons until she felt ready. In fact, when she left the studio, she would leave the new work turned to the wall.

The third boundary was for her mind. Having discussed the differences between her creative source and the part of her mind that put others' opinions first, we planned that on entering the studio, she would hold the intention of leaving her social mind, along with fear and doubt, at the door, to be picked up again only when she left the studio for the day. Reflective writing at the start of her painting session would help to support this shift.

A month later, she'd moved her studio, and this helped her to bypass her knee-jerk reactions to doubt and fear. She'd taken new risks, and when she looked at what she'd produced, she felt overcome by self-loathing. But although her first impulse was to trash the work, she didn't. She used her reflective journal to write down her thoughts, the emotional and the analytical ones. And when she returned to the painting, she completed it successfully (although, she added, "Others might disagree.") Nevertheless, she felt that she was getting to know her creative process better. But now her new work looked different from the work she'd been exhibiting, and she was anxious about being criticized for her lack of consistency.

We approached the voices of authority in her mind with curiosity. Were their threats and criticisms out of date, or were they warning her of genuine risks? How old did she feel when these inner judges appeared? Like many of us, when inner judges were at their harshest, she felt about five or six years old. As a child, she had learned to be meek and compliant to avoid the scathing and mocking remarks of a group of older girls at school. I suggested that she might thank her inner critics for helping her to dodge some of the bullying in the past while recognizing that the threat was outdated, which meant that she could now give the critics some time off and begin to reclaim her own authority.

We looked at how she felt about her lack of formal art training and talked about the positives: the motivation and self-reliance it had taken to assemble her informal but custom-made art education and her breadth of experience in life and work. Indeed, she began to see the benefits of her unorthodox path. Then, where she'd identified real gaps, I asked her how she might fill them.

She yearned for an artist peer group and decided to start meeting fellow artists by attending a weekly life drawing group.

Halfway through the block of coaching sessions she wrote that she was becoming much quicker at catching the inner critics at work, had made a shift from feeling caught in the bullied child response, and had told the 'big girls' in her mind that she wasn't going to buy their cruel comments. In addition, she found that she was enjoying taking creative risks.

Continuing to challenge the imagined opinions of authority, she gathered a list of rules about making art, decided whether each rule was helpful or outdated, and chose which rules to break. She wrote letters—not for sending—in the voice of her inner six-year-old, to the girls who had undermined her as a child. She also acknowledged those who had supported her creative self.

Over the next few sessions, including email work, we explored her anxiety about consistency. She was concerned that having 'disconnected work' would prevent her from gaining respect within the art world, and prevent sales. We agreed that every 'expert' was likely to have her or his own unique opinion and that imagining that they were all right could only create confusion. However, she could show her new work to the gallery owners who were selling her traditional paintings and ask whether they would consider exhibiting the new ones. If not, she could look for other galleries that might be a better fit.

However, Gina recognized that she also needed to work on clarifying her own values and explore whether consistency was intrinsically important to her. By reflecting on her most successful work and work by the artists that she most admired, she was able to make a list of what she valued, taking into consideration her feeling responses, her thoughts and ideas, and the bodily sensations they sparked.

She became more confident working in both her traditional and experimental directions, but she still worried about audience reaction. We planned how she might talk about her work in a forthcoming open studio day, changing her statement from, "My work looks disconnected," to "I've been taking more risks with my work recently." She prepared phrases that would help people connect with the new ideas and identified a supportive friend with whom she could practice.

Her day was a success. Nevertheless, she still fretted about the impulses of her butterfly mind to visit multiple ideas and possibilities. I asked her to imagine the opposite situation—having no ideas. This reframing allowed her to see her so-called problem as an unlimited supply of inspiration. I suggested looking for examples of respected artists who have explored multiple directions. And although she could use her list of criteria if she had to choose among ideas, she also began to look for connections between her themes.

We also worked on managing her butterfly mind, on focusing and grounding. We chose a method of organizing ideas lists, one list of current projects and another longer one of ideas for keeping on the back burner, accessible but out of sight. In session, she enjoyed an exercise I'd suggested for grounding herself whenever she sensed she was too lost in her head. The exercise involved bringing her attention to her feet and then to a few inches beneath them, allowing time to enjoy the connection.

The next time we met, she had been disappointed by a rejection from an open exhibition, and we considered how she might create a recovery ritual, going from simply giving space and time for the first emotional impact of a setback, to observing her reactions and noticing and challenging negative thoughts, to then clearing and relaxing emotional and physical tensions before planning to move forward.

By the end of this block of sessions, Gina was bringing more of herself into her paintings, had produced a body of work with new subject matter, and could better handle other people's opinions. She had taken a part-time job in a gallery, which helped her to relate to the gallery owner as an individual, reduced the pressure to sell, and allowed her to relax more in the making of the work. She had firsthand evidence of increased resilience: despite another rejection, she had remained positive about the painting in question, going on to enter it into a second exhibition. She was working on a large commission, sales were going well, and she could now see and describe the relationships between the different strands of her work, works that had previously seemed disconnected to her.

Learning Points

1. When you consider boundary issues, think about them in terms of physical workspace, the creation of 'sacred, time, and between the socialized mind and the creative inner world.
2. A reflective journal can help movement forward from initially overwhelming emotional reactions and for challenging beliefs or negative conclusions.
3. Recognizing that those we regard as authority figures are unlikely to all be in agreement opens up the possibility of relating to those individuals with whom we share values.

Self-Coaching Questions

1. Have you found ways to avoid intrusions of unwanted 'guests,' real or imagined, into your workspace or time?
2. What would be your ideal ritual for making the crossing of the threshold from the social mind to your creative inner world?
3. Could any of your outdated or one-sided narratives about yourself, rules, or 'authority' be rewritten?

About Elise V. Allan

Elise V. Allan's decision to train as a creativity coach stemmed from a desire to bring over 40 years' experience as an artist and a long-term interest in personal development together. Working as a part-time art school lecturer since the early 1990s, her interest in supporting student motivation led to working with a research partner on creating a series of workshops on how best to enhance and sustain motivation. A CCA-certified creativity coach, Elise can be contacted at www.elisevallan-creativitycoaching.co.uk/contact. Her paintings can be seen at www.elisevallan.com.

A Meaningful Writing Career

4

How Values and Creative Work Can Align

Gina Edwards

I'm leaving a regional writer's meeting when a spritely 40-ish woman stops me. "I *need* to talk to *you*." Her directness catches me off guard. I know about Cicely—that she's one of the few writers in the community making a living from her writing. But I don't know her. "I want to shift my career." She sounds anxious but determined. "I need you to help me."

Before I can form a response, she continues, "I *know* you can help. You're a creativity coach, right?" She leans toward me and whispers, "I've wanted to make this shift for a long time but haven't known what to do first."

I wonder what she means by "shift." Is she looking to cross genres? In the past, publishers didn't want writers to deviate from the writing they'd become "known" for, but today, self-publishing allows authors to cross genres at will.

"I'm really good at planning," she adds. "And I can get things done, but I know I need . . . some guidance."

Often, writers come to me with a sense that they need "something," but they're unsure about the nature of support that would best serve them.

Cicely continues, "I'm efficient and meet deadlines. And with someone like you helping me stay on course, I'll get there even quicker."

Her enthusiasm is encouraging. She knows her strengths; we wouldn't need to spend the first few coaching sessions parsing those out in order to set a direction for her. From what she's told me so far, it seems we'd primarily do a series of accountability sessions. To be sure, though, I need to understand more about this "shift" she's referring to. I want to be clear about the end goal she sees for herself.

"What kind of shift are you looking to make?" I finally ask.

"These books I write don't get seen," she says. She goes on to explain that her projects are mostly coffee-table books, beautiful books she's written—and written well, she emphasizes—about the histories of influential families and regional institutions. They hire her to create these books, which primarily are given as gifts to family members, key personnel, or boards of directors.

"They're flavored with regional history," she adds. "I'm invisible, though. I need to get myself out there more." She pauses. "And I need to do something more important."

We chat a bit and agree to a time and location for our first session, a cozy coffee shop with a fireplace and comfortable chairs. When we meet, Cicely seems less anxious than when we first met. She says she's excited to get started on her writing career adjustment. She has an English degree from a southern university, and then she decided a few years ago to get an MFA from a private liberal arts college in the northeast.

She speaks about her fellow students and professors from the northeast with admiration, listing their credentials and accomplishments. Then she lays out her thoughts about the literary magazines she wants to approach. We discuss topics she's considering. "I don't write about myself, though," she adds.

We spend an hour reviewing her publications list and prioritizing topics. We schedule to meet once a month for six months, with email check-ins between. I set the deadlines she requested. We establish a tracking system for her submissions.

During those first six months, Cicely is deadline-driven, productive, and self-motivated—just as she'd described herself. Each time she finishes a story, we review her topics and identify more publications for her to write toward.

At every meeting, she updates me on her northeastern colleagues, the kinds of projects they're doing, where their work has been accepted, how prestigious the publications are. She stays on course with her goals for writing and submitting well-crafted essays. But with each meeting, her enthusiasm diminishes.

Over the course of an additional six months, we do regular email and phone check-ins. At her request, we meet twice face to face. She continues with her priority list of topics; together we maintain her submissions tracking system. She achieves every deadline. It's a slow process, but she has reasonable expectations that the shift will take a while.

After 12 months, she's comfortable with the writing and submission process we've developed and asks if we can meet on an as-needed basis. I note a low energy from her that's uncharacteristic but assure her I'm available when she needs me.

I don't hear from Cicely for four months. Then she calls to see if we can meet; she's not moving forward the way she'd hoped. Even on the phone, I can tell she isn't her usual animated and enthusiastic self.

When we meet, she updates me on her MFA cohorts first, as usual. Then she lowers her voice. She's decided to take on another book project to record the history of a prominent local family influential in the growth of the community where she lives. "Since they've been here for four generations, I'll really be able to incorporate regional history into this one." I notice her eyes light up, and she sits taller when she says this.

Wondering whether waiting on responses from the publications about her essays has made her weary or frustrated and if the book project would simply be a distraction from that discomfort, I ask, "How will that affect your plans for the career shift?"

She thinks for a moment. "The book will take a lot of time." Even with this realization, her tone still has a lilt to it. I wait to see if she answers my question, but there's silence. Finally, she says, "But I'm looking forward to immersing myself in the research and having a single, big project to focus on again."

I allow her to sit with her words for a moment. Then I ask, "Are you returning to that type of work because it's comfortable and familiar? Or because you want to?"

She takes in a breath and then speaks slowly. "I can visualize the outcome of the book project."

"There's less unknown," I agree.

She looks in my eyes, and I can tell she's thinking deeply. "Yes, but it feels right, too."

I give her time with her thoughts. After a few moments, she shrugs and says nothing. I think I see tears welling.

"Cicely, why do you write?" I ask.

She's quiet, looking into the fire, occasionally glancing up as coffee drinkers pass. Finally, she says, "I want to write books that matter."

"Tell me more," I say.

"I like creating interesting stories out of things people think are mundane or look at as historical *facts* and might normally avoid. I love to weave interesting narratives out of seemingly dull topics . . . like John McPhee. He's the master." She shifts in her chair and then shakes her head. "So many authors want to write their own stories, and apparently that's what the publications want. I'm more enthralled with other people's stories . . . and they need to be told."

In those words, I sense an underlying comparison of herself with the fellow MFA students she has bragged about each time we've met.

I lean toward her. "May I ask two questions?"

"Of course."

"They aren't easy ones, so it's okay if you don't answer right away."

She nods.

"What values and beliefs underpin your writing?"

She wrinkles her forehead. "I'll have to think about that one."

"Sure. You don't have to answer today. The other question: how do you measure your success as a writer?"

"I never thought about that."

"Please do. Take a few days or as long as you need. But do give me an answer from your heart."

She agrees to email me after spending time with the questions I've posed. Two weeks later, I receive this:

> I write true stories because real life fascinates me. People have value and have something important to say. I want to give them a voice and make it authentic to them, whether that's me authoring or ghostwriting. I don't care whether I'm 'seen' or not.
>
> I want my readers to discover things, expand their knowledge of their own heritage, their personal history, and perhaps bring them healing as well. I want to give those gifts.
>
> I'm successful when I'm doing work that feels true to myself rather than what academia or culture dictate. When I feel satisfied that I'm doing writing that *matters* and when, along the way, I make unexpected discoveries about my subjects and myself, then I know I'm doing it the right way *for me*.
>
> I want to do more of the intimate family portraits that fascinate me; their stories need to be told. It's time for me to focus on long-form narrative—immersion work: books.

And so, we came full circle. Cicely returned to the work she loved but had abandoned because others made her believe it wasn't important enough or prestigious enough. When she examined the values and beliefs she held about her life, her work, her community and its history, she was able to define the path that mattered to her.

Learning Points

1. Looking at others to find meaning in your own work causes "comparison-itis," which can get you off course from the work that really matters to you.

2. Take time to think clearly about the values and beliefs that serve you and your writing life.
3. Define success for yourself rather than using someone else's definition; create your writing life on your own terms.

Self-Coaching Questions

1. What core values and beliefs underpin your writing practice?
2. How are they reflected in your work and writing practice, and how could you incorporate them more?
3. How do you measure your success as a writer?

About Gina Edwards

Gina Edwards is a retreat leader, a certified creativity coach, and a book editor. She is also a writer, so she's intimately familiar with the challenges and elation that come with being one. She supports all writers—published and aspiring—who want to write as an act of courageous and necessary self-expression. Walking the writer's path hand in hand with her clients and students, she helps them establish a writing practice and define a creative life on their own terms. You can connect with Gina at www.AroundTheWritersTable.com.

A Musician's 'Impossible Dream'

5

Overcoming Stage Fright With Creativity Coaching

Nick Lazaris

The message on my office voicemail seemed urgent in tone. Julie had attended my recent workshop *Overcoming Performance Anxiety* and desired to speak to me regarding her husband Jim, an accountant for whom she was desperately seeking help. Although Jim worked in a large accounting firm and was very successful in his 25-year career, he was struggling with an unresolved issue since his days as a performing musician in college. Would I, as a creativity coach, be willing to see Jim and help him through his current challenge? I said I would love to meet him and set up our first coaching session together.

In our introductory meeting, Jim shared with me his history with performance anxiety and the moment he had decided to move away from his music. As he described it, he had been on track toward becoming a successful professional French horn player after college. At the top of his class in his skills as a musician, it seemed as though nothing would stop him on the career trajectory he was on. Nothing, that is, until he stepped on stage for his final college senior recital.

As he walked towards the chair in the middle of the large, empty stage, he looked out toward the crowd, including family, friends, and peers, that was there to see his final performance as a college student.

Eyes were also on him from the jury of his professors who would grade him one final time and send him on his way to his career in the performing arts. As he glanced around the hall, he noticed that his breathing was becoming shorter and faster. He began to take in large gulps of air as his mind started racing toward thoughts of "What if I can't breathe? What if everyone can see that I am getting nervous? What if I blow my performance?"

Jim's anxiety began to escalate as he sat on the chair to begin his performance. What had begun as excitement turned into fear and physical tightness as he gripped his instrument and began to play. More and more negative thoughts replaced what would normally be a feeling of focused presence while performing music he had played hundreds of times before. As his mind and body continued to focus on his anxiety, the unthinkable happened—he froze in the middle of the piece.

His heart pounding, he somehow gained enough presence to complete his piece, stood, bowed, and walked off stage in complete humiliation. "What just happened?" Jim thought to himself. As much as he tried to put this experience into the category of 'everyone has a bad performance once in a while,' he began to fear that it might happen again. Sure enough, after graduation and as he embarked upon his career as a musician, the performance anxiety did not stop. In fact, it became increasingly worse as his fear of freezing on stage became an obsession, eventually causing him to stop playing professionally. In time, he put away his French horn and stopped playing even for his own enjoyment.

What better way to not face his fear than to stop doing the thing that led to his severe anxiety and panic. For Jim, it was time to get a 'real job,' one that was safe and without the possibility of failure. It was time to move on with his life. His life as a performer was over, and for the next 23 years, he did not perform again.

Fast forward to the week before I met Jim. He had received a phone call from his daughter, a vocalist in New York, who was coming to his California hometown in five months to headline an orchestral concert. She had asked Jim for something that both of them had dreamed about for many years, performing a duet together.

His daughter's desire for her father to accompany her on stage with his French horn brought back memories of his days of severe anxiety and panic. He told me that his immediate reflex was to turn down this great opportunity because his performing days were over.

I shared with Jim that I specialized in helping performers overcome their fear of stage fright and that I believed I could help him. He said that he found it hard to believe, in fact "impossible," that he could overcome his anxiety but was willing to try as the opportunity was such a significant one for him. We agreed to meet in person every week, with some email support between our sessions. Because the concert was only five months away, we would begin our work together the following week.

Our focus for the next weeks would be on both the cognitive as well as the physical side of approaching his anxiety. The initial goal of any type of change, I said, is 'awareness,' that is, an understanding of what is going on and what the path is to overcome the challenge. I explained that while under stress, real or imagined, there are several things that can affect our performance. These include mental effects such as doubts, self-criticism, negative self-talk, and a lack of focus and concentration. In addition, there are physical effects that begin to affect our performance, with adrenaline starting to kick in, causing our muscles to tighten up and our breathing to change. During these changes, we can begin to feel alone with our feelings, further escalating the stress and anxiety.

Jim began to understand how much the mind and the body are connected and that when we are afraid of a negative thing happening (such as freezing or blanking out on stage), our body follows such thinking and prepares us for something that appears dangerous. Our physiology changes to get ready for the thing we are afraid of. The vicious cycle begins, and our initial stress turns into ever deepening and escalating anxiety. For Jim to be able to perform with his daughter, he realized that he must learn skills to 'slow down' his mind and body. He told me he was ready, and we moved forward by creating the following 'road map' of principles and skills that would move him toward his goal of performing on stage again.

Jim's Performance Anxiety Road Map

Step 1. *Take slow, deep, and focused breaths*—Focused, abdominal breathing was one of the most powerful and important tools Jim learned to apply as he practiced his performance. Throughout each day leading up to the concert, he would practice three or four focused breaths, each time becoming more able to slow down his feelings of anxiety and stress when needed.

Step 2. *Identify and practice positive self-talk*—Jim began to monitor how he talked to himself prior to and during a performance and whether his self-talk was positive or negative. He learned the practice of 'thought stopping' whenever he had an anxiety-producing thought. He listened for the "What if's?" and replaced them with "So what!" Slowly, he began to be aware of his anxiety-provoking thoughts and replaced them with positive statements.

Step 3. *Practice positive mental rehearsal*—Jim discovered that in the past, he had been anticipating that he would freeze on stage and would then experience anxiety as a result of this kind of visualization. We worked on a daily program of positive mental rehearsal of his upcoming performance going well, without any debilitating anxiety.

Step 4. *Relax your muscles to reduce stress*—Progressive muscle relaxation, practiced and combined with deep breathing, allowed Jim to relax, take control of his body, and feel confident that he would perform well.

Step 5. *Learn to center to perform your best*—Centering, as Jim discovered, is a focusing strategy that originated in the martial arts and that, when practiced and applied to any performance situation in which one feels pressure, can channel energy productively in a performance. Soon, Jim was practicing centering every day.

After five months of our coaching work together, Jim expressed a new confidence that he would be able to perform on stage again. Just days before the concert, he told me that he knew that he could do this and thanked me for helping him take charge of his playing again—it was as if he had rediscovered an old friend in his French horn.

The day of the concert, I received a message from Jim accompanied by a video of his performance with his daughter. It was a moment of joy that I, as a creativity coach, would not soon forget as I watched him play his French horn beautifully alongside his daughter.

It was days later that I received this message from Jim that summarized our work together:

> The day of the performance we made our way to the front of the stage—I was completely calm, confident, and in control ("in the moment," as you would label it). The performance went flawlessly, and I was able to thoroughly enjoy the moment and feel very proud of my performance. This was one of the most fulfilling experiences I can ever remember. I don't know where this will go, but I do know that the performance door is now open again, and I can feel free to walk through it if I desire to.

Jim had, indeed, achieved his 'impossible dream.'

Learning Points

1. No matter how 'impossible' you might feel that a creative or performance opportunity is out of reach, never give up hope that you have the potential to achieve your dreams.

2. Seek out guidance when you feel 'stuck.' You do not have to take your creative journey alone. Allow another person to help you create the awareness and skills required to move forward toward your creative goals.
3. The bad news is that creative anxiety is in your head. The good news is that creative anxiety is in your head! Yes, you can learn to *take charge of your fears* and create amazing things to share with the world!

Self-Coaching Questions

1. Have you identified the fears that are paralyzing and keeping you from letting your creativity be fully expressed? Are you allowing yourself to become fully aware of these fears rather than pushing them aside?
2. What do you tell yourself that blocks you from creating your best work? Do you find yourself making excuses or even lying to yourself about what you are capable of? Is it time to step out into the 'unknown' and take the necessary risks to express your authentic creative self?
3. What specific skills from the Anxiety Road Map would make a difference *today* if you were to start applying them when you feel anxious?

About Nick Lazaris

As a performance psychologist and creativity coach, Dr. Nick Lazaris has specialized for 38 years in helping performing artists, business professionals, entrepreneurs, and creatives overcome public speaking anxiety, stage fright, and anxiety as an artist or writer. Dr. Nick coaches those who desire to increase their self-confidence, overcome fear, and perform and create at or near their personal best. He is available for a limited amount of coaching and consulting engagements via phone, Skype, Zoom, or in person. You can contact Dr. Nick at nick@drnicklazaris.com or go to www.drnicklazaris.com to receive your free Performance Anxiety Road Map, *Overcome Stage Fright Forever.*

Della's Dream Comes True

6

Subpersonality Work With a Blocked Writer

Marj Penley

Della, a woman in her late 60s with gray hair tightly curled in a hundred (or so it seemed) tiny coils, told me in our first session that she'd always wanted to be a fiction writer, but she had never even started writing.

"Now as I see my life slipping away over the horizon, I really want to write. I don't want to die without having written a single thing—not even one short story."

She told me that she had read Stephen King's book *On Writing* and had followed his recommendations to read a lot. When it came to his other recommendation, to write a lot, she hadn't done any at all.

To become more aware of the parts or subpersonalities that might be blocking her creativity, I asked her if she would be willing to try a guided imagery exercise.

She was very willing and, in just a couple minutes, she was lying comfortably against the pillows on the back of the couch. She closed her eyes and, with a small amount of guidance from me, allowed herself to slip into a deep state of relaxation.

I invited her to imaginatively climb a mountain, which she would see to her left, and at the top of the mountain she would become aware of a building with the sign reading "**Subpersonalities**" above the door.

I asked her to open the door and describe whatever subpersonality she encountered.

As soon as she opened the door, she saw a large spider with hairy legs and sharp, pointed teeth. She said his hairy legs would grab her, and then he'd sink his sharp teeth into her arm, injecting his poison.

When I asked her about the poison, she said, "Oh, lots of poisonous words. He says stuff like, 'You ain't got no talent' or 'You're no writer.'"

"Does this spider remind you of anyone you have known?"

She thought for a moment and then said, "Oh, yes, it reminds me of my kindergarten teacher. I remember painting Lincoln's arms blue in a painting, and she ripped it up, saying, 'Whoever heard of such nonsense!'"

"I tried to tell her that I painted his arms blue because I knew he came from a cold part of the country and, so, he was probably cold. I knew my own arms turned blue whenever I was cold. But she didn't listen and just shredded the painting even more."

At first Della wanted to kill the spider, but I suggested she just put it in some kind of container for now. I explained that someday she might want to know more about this poisonous part.

I asked Della to open the door again and this time call out another subpersonality that would support and encourage her writing.

She quickly exclaimed, "Oh, I know who that is—that's my Aunt Kate. She always supported and encouraged me to learn new things."

"Would you be willing to invite her to come out of the building holding all your subpersonalities?"

"Oh, yes."

Della soon announced, "I asked her to come out, and she came out right away. Didn't have to ask her twice. She just she gave me a big hug."

"Ask her how she can support your writing."

Della nodded, and in a few moments said, "She is encouraging me to write about my life experiences. She says she'd be there, whispering in my ear many things I may have forgotten."

"How does that sound to you?"

"It sounds just great."

"Then why don't you find a way to say good-bye to your Aunt Kate and invite her to go back into the 'subpersonalities' building. Once you are sure she is inside, you can close the door."

When Della opened her eyes, she said, "That was the best thing—the very best thing. I just want to go home and write. There's so much I have to say."

But when Della returned for her next session, she hadn't written a thing. When I asked her about it, she said, "Oh, I just couldn't think of the right words."

"Just the right words," I repeated. "Any chance you have a perfectionist subpersonality lurking around?"

"Oh, I don't know. Maybe. I do like to arrange my things in the kitchen in just the right order. I toss out any vegetables with even very small brown spots. I certainly never want to make any mistakes in my sewing." She paused for a moment, thinking. "I guess you might be right. I do seem to have a perfectionist subpersonality."

"Well, the perfectionist subpersonality can actually be useful when you're polishing the final draft of your writing. But you don't want him around at all in the beginning. Not for rough drafts. So, what can we do with this perfectionist part?"

"Maybe I can just put him in a box. This box, though, will need a lid so that I can remove it easily when I need his input for the last draft."

"I know I have a critical part, too," she added. "It can be pretty fearsome critical. I need a box with a tight-fitting lid for him, too. Then I can let them both out when I get to the last draft of the story. That is, when I need their input. Does that seem to be right?"

"Yes, you are certainly catching on quickly to this method of working with subpersonalities, Della."

"What's the next step? What should I do next?"

"Well, Della, how would it be if you started a daily writing practice? Take a pad of paper and a pen. Write for 15 to 30 minutes nonstop. You can write about anything you'd like. You want to just keep the pen moving across the paper. Don't worry about grammar or spelling or, for that matter, don't worry about anything. Just write. How does that sound to you?"

"Not great. I have so much to do, you know. All the cleaning and washing and ironing."

"Ironing?" I asked. "Did you say 'ironing'?"

"Yes, I iron every day—my blouses, my husband's shirts, his underwear, the sheets, and pillowcases and . . ."

I interrupted her. "What would happen if you didn't iron this week?"

"Probably nothing too terrible."

"So, would you be willing to write for the 15 to 30 minutes each day?"

"Yes, I can do that. I can write instead of ironing. I can iron out all my ideas," she said with an impish smile on her face.

I laughed. "That's a good image. 'Iron out all your ideas.' What do you think? Are you ready to write? Can you make a commitment to write every day?"

Della beamed. "You betcha. I'm on my way, aren't I?"

When Della came for her next session, she still hadn't done any writing even though she had made a commitment to do so before she left the office the week before.

"What happened, Della? What stopped you from some daily writing?"

Della seemed unusually quiet, sitting on just the edge of the couch.

"What are you experiencing, Della? What's going on?"

"I took out a scrapbook I made in grammar school, and there on the first page was a photo of my kindergarten teacher. She was frowning in the photo, and a flood of memories came back to me. I think she criticized everything I did—my drawing, my handwriting, my way of jumping rope, everything."

"What do you want or need?"

"I need for her to leave me alone."

"Can you pretend that your kindergarten teacher is sitting in the chair over there?"

"I guess I can. She has been dead for over 20 years, though."

"That may be true. But, nevertheless, she has been an ongoing influence in your life. We want to change that. Now tell her to stop criticizing you."

Della said, speaking to the imaginary teacher in the chair, "You've been criticizing me my whole life. Please stop it."

"That's good, Della. Can you say it a little louder? Also, please drop the 'please'."

Della took a deep breath and shouted, "You've been criticizing me my whole life. I always hear your voice in my head. Now stop it! Just stop it!"

"Did she hear you?" I asked.

Della nodded.

For the next couple weeks, we focused some more on the kindergarten teacher. Della made life-size drawings of the teacher on newsprint and tore them up. As she shredded them, she released many of her pent-up emotions of anger and sadness.

Sometimes she saw the teacher as the spider and made drawings of the spider, tearing them up as well.

Finally, Della imagined putting the teacher in a boat and sending her to North Korea.

Della began writing, and soon she had written several stories. She quite consciously kept the perfectionist part and the critical part in their boxes until she was working on her final drafts. Then she would let them out of their boxes to provide her with input. Most of the time, she followed their advice, and as a result, her stories became better and better.

Before Della died, she had written several short stories and four complete novels and was awarded two literary prizes.

Learning Points

1.   A method for discovering subpersonalities: the guided fantasy.

2. A method for working with subpersonalities: the chair technique.
3. A method for releasing emotions: the use of art supplies. For example, drawing on newsprint and then tear it up passionately.

Self-Coaching Questions

1. What subpersonalities are preventing you from doing your creative work?
2. What subpersonalities are supporting you in doing your creative work?
3. What methods can you use for containing, controlling, or directing a subpersonality?

About Marj Penley

Marj Penley, a licensed CA therapist for more than 30 years and a CCA certified creativity coach, loves to support, guide, enliven, inspire, and empower people worldwide. With the background of an ESL teacher and certified in cross-cultural communication, she has worked with people from Japan, Korea, and many other countries. She has been developing her own skills in the fields of writing, Japanese brush painting, watercolors, and ceramics. Marj welcomes email at kreativecoaching@frontier.com. To learn more about her coaching, classes, and workshops visit her website at www.marjpenley.com.

A Change of Scenery May Be Just the Ticket   **7**

How Creativity and Travel Can Help Reinvent Midlife

Jan Moore

A group of eight women, age 50+, came together for a one-day university continuing education workshop to learn how to reinvent themselves in midlife. The women included an executive, a fast food worker, and a teacher. Each person expressed a burning desire to travel along with a fear that it was not financially possible.

During the workshop, the women looked at numerous ways to save or make money after leaving a full-time job, received tips on affordable travel, and plotted their dream destinations on a map. They were introduced to the self-employment stories of several women who used their creativity to make successful midlife career changes. The group then brainstormed ideas for each group member.

Women are leaving their careers, willingly or unwillingly and asking themselves, "What's next?" Workshop participants said retirement is not an option because of financial worries or a need for continued purpose and meaning. The group explored how travel can be affordable and can fast track career reinvention. We looked at three examples of women who have already reinvented themselves while travelling and how each had used her creativity.

Patricia B. is the owner of a small shop that carries handcrafted items from around the world. During her travels, Patricia buys items from local crafts workers to stock her store. This helps fund her travels.

Before owning the shop, Patricia worked as a bartender, studied corporate communication, became a single parent, and refinished furniture and sold it in another small shop prior to moving about 600 miles to her current home.

Doreen P. is a writer who loves chocolate. She started visiting places that produce good-quality chocolate and writing about them. She now has a blog devoted to chocolate and is often invited to locations around the globe where she gets to sample their chocolate and write about it. She wrote an award-winning book about chocolate, guides chocolate tastings, and has plans to lead other women on chocolate tours.

Doreen has been a nonfiction writer for several decades. She has written for numerous publications. She followed her passion for chocolate around the world and is now known as the Chocolate Queen. Her love of chocolate funds her travels.

Anne M. gave up photojournalism for a traditional career in software development. She became increasingly saddened by her negative view of the world around her. In her 40s, she decided to sell her home and business and head out on the road with her husband and dogs in an RV. She decided to only take pictures of anything she deemed beautiful. No more depressing photos for her.

Anne is now an accomplished photographer who travels the world with her camera and teaches others how to take a good photo. She now lives a happier, more fulfilling life on the road and earns her living from photography.

The workshop participants enjoyed learning from these examples, and it got them thinking about ideas for themselves. The workshop participants discussed three main ways women are reinventing themselves.

Path #1: Creativity

As women age, we are aware of time speeding up and increasingly being drawn toward using our creativity as a way to find our voice and express it. Many of us have not had time to make full use of our creativity—until now.

Women who have made a satisfying midlife career change say that creativity is their "secret sauce."

The group discussed that women who heed the call of creativity are rewarded with more fun, physical and mental well-being, and connection with others and enjoy having an outlet for self-expression. They want to experiment with creative mediums until they find one that best fits their needs.

Path #2: Entrepreneurship

Women age 55+ are the fastest growing group of entrepreneurs. The women discussed a growing disillusion with big business. They feel the pinch of age discrimination and realize if they want a "job for life," they'd better create it for themselves. They believe this would give them a chance to create the lifestyle they want and fulfilling work to support it.

The group discussed how self-employment provides the opportunity to express more of who they are and to use their favorite skills and is a chance to use more of their creativity. The workshop participants understand that creativity and self-employment often walk hand in hand.

Path #3: Travel

The #1 dream of many Boomer women is to have more time for travel and adventure. This was the primary reason for the participants attending the workshop. The women said they are tired of working most of the year and squeezing in a two- or three-week vacation. They crave new experiences and want to exchange having more stuff for more adventure.

The workshop participants felt that those who combine travel with creativity and entrepreneurship can enjoy the best of all three worlds. The group discussed how women are taking their employment ideas on the road with them and using travel to learn from other cultures and creative entrepreneurs around the world.

The group explored the most popular ways to make travel affordable. Many women are choosing to live part time or full time in a low-cost country such as Thailand, Portugal, or Mexico. The most popular way to save money is to house or pet sit because it offers free accommodation around the world. The group was intrigued to learn that those who travel by RV can camp for free on public lands. This is especially popular with snowbirds visiting California or Arizona. They discussed other options to save on accommodation, including house swaps and homestays.

We discussed how artists provide great examples of reinvention. Many writers and painters have spent time in Paris, and the city inspired their muse. We don't need to apply for an artist-in-residence program; we can create our own.

Visiting local markets, taking a class, speaking with local artisans, and exploring art galleries and museums can open up a whole new world. We also discussed how it's easier to try on a new persona in a place where no one knows your name or has a preconceived idea about what's possible for you.

The women felt corporate culture tends to discourage asking, "Why do we do things this way?" They know artists explore outside the boundaries and test out new ways of seeing and being in the world and travel provides a similar opportunity.

At the end of the workshop, participants were asked for feedback. This is what they had to say:

Kathryn said, "I attended this workshop only a few weeks after finishing an 11-month solo tour of Europe, Africa, and Asia. I'm a confident, creative, and curious older woman traveler who did her first solo trip at the age of 17 to Europe. This workshop gave me some very tangible tips and tools on how to save and even make money while traveling. It was so inspiring that I've begun planning my next adventure with a new approach on traveling."

Laurel said, "I can recapture my courage and sense of adventure. There are options to cut travel costs plus create extra income during traveling. No more excuses! Life is too short to wait for a moment to arrive. Live the moment!"

Beatrice said, "All is possible when you have the tools to achieve your travel goals. Also, it makes you reconnect with your forgotten dreams."

The workshop participants are looking forward to using their creativity during their future travels. They know it takes courage to walk through fear and self-doubt. Each participant took a sheet of brainstormed ideas home with her—with an intention to do more research and put a midlife reinvention plan into action. I hope they keep in touch to let me know about their midlife reinvention.

Exploring your creativity can help you find a tribe of like-minded folks who are on a similar path. Affordable travel can speed up the process. Purpose and meaning are the keys to happiness. Retirement is out. Reinvention is in.

> There is a fountain of youth: It is your mind, your talents, the creativity you bring to your life and the lives of people you love. When you learn to tap into this source, you will truly have defeated age.
>
> Sophia Loren

Learning Points

1. The fasted way to reinvent midlife is through travel.
2. You can create your own artist-in-residence program.
3. Visiting a low-cost country makes it more affordable to explore your creativity and self-employment options.

Self-Coaching Questions

1. If you could try on a different persona when you travel, what would that look like?
2. Which of the three examples of midlife reinvention resonate with you? Patricia? Doreen? Anne?
3. Is there a country you believe could really spark your creativity and imagination?

About Jan Moore

Jan Moore transitioned from a full-time job as a career counselor to a midlife reinvention coach when she wrote the book *Work on Your Own Terms in Midlife & Beyond*. She has an MA in leadership & training and is certified as a retirement coach, senior advisor, and life skills coach. Jan knows our inner souls crave expression, and midlife is the time to let our creativity out. Expressing it is good for our health in body, mind and spirit. Get a copy of *10 Delightful Ways Travel Can Change Your Life* plus other resources on midlife reinvention via travel and creativity at www.WorkOnYourOwnTerms.com.

An Artist Prepares   **8**

How Dreams Can Come True Sooner Than You Expect

Sharon Good

When Elizabeth contacted me about coaching, she was the epitome of the starving artist. A sweet, shy young woman, she had come from her home in the Midwest to the "big city" in her 20s to launch her career as an artist.

Elizabeth had gotten her BFA from a local state university. After graduation, she had continued living with her family and took low-level jobs as a cashier or store clerk to save money to move to a big city where there would be greater opportunities to build her career and promote her work as an artist.

She had researched several cities and chosen the one that appealed to her the most. Her family supported her, but they had three more kids to raise and put through school, so they couldn't offer her much in the way of financial assistance. She scrimped and saved for two years and finally had enough saved to make the move.

When Elizabeth got to the city, she found a cheap apartment on the outskirts of the city and landed a "glamour job" with a prestigious museum, but in truth, the work was tedious and paid very little, and she was barely making ends meet. Her artwork had gone by the wayside, and she had completely fallen off the path toward her creative goals. She didn't have many friends and couldn't afford to go out with them anyway, so she felt lonely and isolated. Not a happy picture.

In desperation, Elizabeth decided to seek out a creativity coach to help her get back on track. When I interviewed her to see if we were a good match as coach and client, she admitted to me that there were months where she had to choose between eating and paying the rent. Even so, she was committed to moving ahead with her work as an artist and willing to (somehow) pay for coaching.

As I talked with Elizabeth and pondered her situation, I saw that she was truly sincere. I sensed that we would work well together, and I wanted to take her on as a client. But I couldn't, in good conscience, take money from her when she was already living on the edge just to pay for her basic needs. So, I decided to take her on as a "pro bono" (nonpaying or "scholarship") client.

Now, pro bono clients are not known for their reliability, but Elizabeth was a model coaching client. She showed up to every session, eager and ready to work, and did the action steps she agreed to, and then some.

We began by looking at her long-term goals. She wanted to be a successful artist, but more than that, her big dream was to open a retreat center where artists of all types could come and stay for a reasonable rate and spend some time focusing on their creative work. It seemed that the immediate focus was for Elizabeth to get established as a professional artist herself, so she could build on her reputation as a basis for launching the retreat center, as well as building up some savings to fund the project. At this point, she was just starting her own art career, so this dream seemed to be far into the future, maybe 20 or 30 years ahead.

In the present moment, Elizabeth was feeling discouraged because she couldn't even afford to buy art materials, and she had stopped doing her own work. The immediate goal was to find a way to get her creating again, as well as finding ways to increase her income.

Elizabeth managed to scrounge up a few supplies and found objects, and she set a goal to create one small painting or collage a week. This new goal energized and encouraged her, and she began making art again. She showed her work to some of her coworkers at the museum, who loved her work, and she began selling some small pieces, which enabled her to buy more supplies.

As she began building up some inventory, Elizabeth decided to start a store on Etsy and sell her work. She was pleasantly surprised and delighted to find that her pieces were selling well, allowing her to continue creating more, and bigger, pieces. Her confidence grew, and she started experimenting more with her artistic style. She tried different modalities and styles to see what she most enjoyed and did well, as well as what her market was interested in buying.

As Elizabeth's income began to increase, she was able to cover her basic expenses and buy more art materials and still have a little left over. She started getting out more and meeting up with work friends to go to dinner or a movie. Having more social contact also put her in a better state of mind, and she was starting to enjoy life more.

Another one of Elizabeth's goals was to get connected in the art world. Now that she had some disposable income, she had the funds to network in art circles and visit galleries and openings, where she could make contacts to promote her work in the future. She made one strong connection with Amanda, a gallery owner who loved her work and saw the potential for selling it as Elizabeth continued to develop her craft.

So, the short-term goal of getting her artwork going was falling into place beautifully. She was even able to start paying for her coaching sessions. The surprise came when the timeline on her long-term dream shortened dramatically.

A few months after we had started coaching, Elizabeth showed up to her session all excited. She had spoken to a good friend back home, Shelley, who was rattling around by herself in a huge house that she had inherited from her grandmother. Shelley had been working as a manager at a local supermarket and was bored and looking for something inspiring to do.

As they talked, the idea of using the house to start an artists' retreat began to take shape. Elizabeth understood what artists needed, and Shelley had taken some college courses in business management. It was a perfect match!

We continued coaching for another month as Elizabeth packed up her things, terminated the lease on her apartment, and gave notice at her job. Even though her coaching goals were still a work in progress, the vision was beginning to come together, and Elizabeth had created a future that was a real possibility that could happen soon rather than 20 years in the future. Her assumption that she needed to create a name for herself and build up her savings first turned out not to be true. We had a joyous, celebratory final session as she prepared to go back home and make her dream a reality.

Epilogue: Elizabeth returned to her hometown and moved in with Shelley. She got a job at the local art supply store to keep some income coming in while she and Shelley planned the retreat center. She continued making art and selling it on Etsy, as well as at the art store and some local boutiques. She kept in touch with Amanda, who encouraged her and promised to show her work when the time was right.

She and Shelley designated four rooms in the house for the retreat center: three bedrooms and a studio. They consulted with a mentor at the local SCORE chapter of the Small Business Association to help them write a business plan and establish the pricing for their guests that was affordable and would also meet their financial goals for the center.

They set up interviews with the owners of other retreat centers and bed and breakfasts to learn more about what they needed to do to run a successful business and to foresee any pitfalls. With a solid plan, they were able to take a small loan from the local banker, who knew them all their lives and was excited to help them get started.

They began decorating the bedrooms and setting up the studio to accommodate artists and writers, using Elizabeth's artwork to brighten up the rooms. They hired a graphic designer to create a logo for them, built a website, and started putting flyers out around town, as well as advertising on the Internet. Elizabeth set up a meeting with the art department at her alma mater, and her favorite professor was thrilled to get the word out in the art and creative writing departments of the university.

Within months, they had their first customers! The last that I heard, the center was thriving, and Elizabeth was able to work on her own art full time, while Shelley managed the business, and they both encouraged other young artists as they created their work.

Learning Points

1. You can apply creativity to the way you live your life, not just your art. How can you creatively go about making things happen in your life and your work?
2. Money is the biggest excuse people have for not following their dreams. Don't let it stop you! When you're fully committed, opportunities will come your way that you couldn't have anticipated.
3. You don't have to do it alone. People love to help, and we work best in communities. Reach out and ask for help.

Self-Coaching Questions

1. If there were no limits, what is your big dream for your creative work and your life? Create a vision for your dream by writing it out or creating a vision board.
2. Where do you feel stuck in your creativity? What are five creative ways that you can get unstuck?
3. Who can you call on to help you achieve your dreams? Commit to reaching out to five contacts this week.

About Sharon Good

Sharon Good, BCC, ACC, CLC, president of Good Life Coaching Inc., based in New York City, brings a rich variety of personal and professional experience to her 20-year career as a life, career, creativity, and retirement coach. With her extensive creative background in publishing, theatre, photography, and graphic design, she coaches artists to achieve their creative and professional goals and helps individuals from all walks of life create fulfilling lives, unique career paths, and enriching retirements. Contact Sharon for individual coaching at her website www.goodlifecoaching.com. Her books are available at www.goodlifepress.com.

Start Where You Are   9
How a Blocked Creativity Coach Finally Wrote Her Case Study

Rachel Marsden

Rachel had been a full-time creativity coach for two years, her practice was thriving, and she was booking many clients by word of mouth. Clients seemed happy and would often rebook her for ongoing sessions.

There was Julia, who was determined to make a living as a photographer. She hired Rachel and poured her heart and soul into building her photography business in a few short months. At first nothing happened. This caused her great distress, and at one point she thought she should quit. However, Rachel supported her in staying steady on her chosen path and helped her understand that this was a normal part of the process. Sure enough, soon all the effort Julia had put in turned into jobs, and she achieved her goal of living off her photography. Julia was thrilled.

There was Sarah, who was painfully confused by her creative urges. She had languished in a dull corporate job for years and yearned for something more. Creativity coaching helped her reframe her situation from a time of despair and overwhelm to seeing this as a time ripe for adventure and exploration. Through coaching, her identity as a creative person was affirmed and she uncovered a passion for fiber art. She joined classes and set up a studio in her home. By her last session with Rachel, she was glowing with happiness, her eyes brimming with tears because not only had she found a joyful outlet for her creative expression but, more important, she'd developed strength and confidence in herself.

Despite these accomplishments and success stories, Rachel felt like a fraud. These successes weren't enough to give her peace of mind about her skills or a sense of being 'good enough' or 'legitimate.' Even the fact that she had a successful practice led her to feel more fraud-like. She had thoughts like: "Oh I just know how to market and have decent business skills," "I'm not really helping them that much," and "They just like me because I'm nice."

Often, she struggled in her own creative work, she had doubts, she didn't finish projects, she took on too many things at once, and sometimes she slipped into states of melancholy. In short, she wasn't a perfect person. She fell into that special downward spiral trap that coaches and therapists can some-times fall into: "If I can't sort my own stuff out, I can't possibly help others? I should know better."

When the opportunity to write a case study for this book arose, she put her hand up immediately. However, as the deadline loomed, she found herself overcome by these doubts and self-criticisms and eventually decided: "I'm not ready for something like this." After a while, Eric sent an email to ask her if she was still participating. It encouraged her and, finally, she decided to face her fears.

Before replying to him, she made a commitment to spend one hour on the case study, even if it made her feel nervous. She told herself she would 'just' spend one hour on it. She would 'just' read the example case studies from the people who had already completed theirs, and she would 'just' jot down some ideas.

The word 'just' helped. Finally, she began. Depending on how it went, at the end of the hour she would reply to Eric's email with a "yes" or a "no." She was so nervous that she couldn't think of what to write about, so she used the Pomodoro technique. The Pomodoro technique is a productivity tool in which you set a timer for 25 minutes and focus on a single task for that time. You take a break for five minutes and then do it again. Although it's generally known as a productivity tool, its secret power is that it beats procrastination and avoidance. This idea of 'it's just 25 minutes' helps to assuage anxieties and resistance toward a task.

She completed the case study readings in the first 25 minutes but still had no idea which client to use for her own case study. It still felt overwhelm-ing. Again, her inner critic was getting the best of her. "You're just not good enough" was the inner critic's summary statement. Yet there was another voice within her that was quietly encouraging. This was her 'inner encour-ager.' It's the voice that gets excited about her ideas, believes in her, likes to have fun, and can have a compassionate laugh at the way the voice of the inner critic was trying to show it cared about Rachel through constant wor-rying.

This encourager knew that she had made a difference in peoples' lives. She could tell by the way their eyes sparkled after they spoke with her, from the emails received later on, and from seeing their creative careers flourish. Sometimes success happened in small ways, sometimes in grand ways. Usually it was through small steps that eventually added up to satisfying changes. She cared about these people, she was dedicated to this work, and this dedication, her inner encourager reminded her, was what was most important.

Another tool she would often use to unblock herself was 'stream of consciousness writing.' This is when you simply write, unfettered, any thoughts that come to your mind. Starting with exactly where you are and how you are feeling is as good a place as any to begin. As soon as she began, a title for her case study came to mind that made her laugh out loud: "Inside the Mind of a Creative Neurotic: How One Coach Overcame Her Blocks to Write Her Case Study."

It sparked some ideas, and she let her stream of consciousness follow those sparks, continuing to laugh out loud as she wrote about herself in third person. It felt absurd, but she was enjoying the process so much so that when the timer marking the second 25 minutes timer went off, she didn't notice and kept writing. She lost track of time. She was now in a flow state and was having a good laugh about it along the way. After all, she was 'just' playing around.

Soon she arrived at the hard part: finishing the draft. Beyond that intimidating step and even more threatening for her anxious side was the step of sharing her case study with Eric. A litany of 'what if's. . . .' and 'who do you think you are. . . ' and 'this is a ridiculous and neurotic idea,' 'I'm embarrassed for you, Rachel,' everyone else who is contributing is so much better than you. . . ' started flooding her brain.

It was too much. Despite the fact that she had been in the flow just 10 seconds before, she stood up and walked away. She needed a break, which she knew meant: 'I feel scared now, and it's getting hard.' Because she was committed to just one hour, she chose to stay steady instead of giving up. She drew on another tool, which she called 'my brain is cooking too hot; I'd better do a physical task to unwind.' This could also be called 'moving into the body.' Rachel could tell that her brain was 'cooking too hot' because her neck, forehead, jaw, and shoulders had become very tense. Even if she was enjoying a process, she knew it was helpful to take time to loosen up.

Tasks such as washing the dishes, taking a shower, going for a walk, or doing some yoga in between creative work can allow your mind and body to unwind and allow for further insights to arise that can help in creative projects. As Rachel moved through some yoga postures, she could calmly observe her inner critic doing its best to protect her by pointing out all the things wrong with her ideas, all the mean and judgmental things people might say and how they would probably be right and how she should just quit now.

However, her inner encourager pointed out that she might not be the only coach or creative person out there who has these feelings. By sharing her inner process, others might feel relieved that they weren't the only ones with doubts, anxieties, and feelings of being a fraud. Perhaps others would find some use in the tools described along the way. And besides, even if people did criticize her, it wouldn't be as bad as a zombie apocalypse.

"True," thought her inner anxious self, "which reminds me, I should probably stock up on tinned food and torch batteries later. Oh dear, I don't even know where my torch is!" Her inner encourager replied, "We'll take care of that later, but for now, let's finish this." Thanks to the creativity coaching skills she'd learned, she returned to the page and made it to the finish line. It was by starting exactly where she was, feeling fraudulent, frightened, and overwhelmed and by using her strengths of curiosity and humor, that Rachel was able to calm her anxieties, unblock herself, draw on tools she already had, and write this case study.

She wrote to Eric and said, 'Yes.'

Learning Points

1. 'Just' begin. Start where you are right now, with what you have available to you and 'just' spend 2, 10, or 20 minutes on your creative project. You 'just' have to do that, nothing else.
2. Humor is a great tool for unblocking. What is there to laugh about in this situation? If there was a fun or absurd solution to your current creative dilemma, what would it be? Interpretive dance? Listening to 80s music? Lying on the floor in a fetal position and crying melodramatically? Find a way to have a laugh. It will reduce tension in your body and help you take your creative block less seriously.
3. Cultivate the voice of your inner encourager. This is the voice that believes in you and is excited about what you do. It sees adventures instead of problems, is compassionate, doesn't care about being 'right' or perfect, and knows you are doing your best. Cultivating this inner voice will help you challenge the opinions of your inner critic and reduce any anxiety you may be feeling.

Self-Coaching Questions

1. What is the tiniest step you could take this minute to move your project forward? Can you open a file, schedule time in your calendar, google a technique, ask someone for coffee? Pick one tiny thing and 'just' take a break from reading this to 'just' do that one thing now.
2. What resources or tools do you already have available to you that you can draw on when you feel too nervous or overwhelmed to move forward? Make a list you can refer to when overwhelm hits.
3. What would make your current creative project more fun? Do that. Or if you can't actually do it, enjoy the fantasy because fantasy often generates creative insight.

About Rachel Marsden

Rachel Marsden is an Australian artist coach living in Berlin, Germany. She works with creative professionals across the spectrum of the creative industries, helping them thrive, prosper, and find fulfillment. Her wild and often anxious creative brain has been her best teacher because it led her to find the tools that help her and now help her clients get out of their heads, past their fears and into their work. More about her coaching can be found at www.thegreatcreativelife.com.

A Filmmaker Returns to Health

10

Creativity Coaching for Overall Wellbeing

Nefeli Soteriou

Johanna was referred to me for my program *Art for Wellbeing*, which I tailor to individuals and to groups. During a session of *Art for Wellbeing*, I create a safe environment for self-expression and use guided exercises I design that are drawn from my professional experience teaching and mentoring diverse populations of all ages, 5–89 years old in music and visual art, such as photography, filmmaking, and design. Artistic skill is not required to participate, only a desire to complete a project and to have some fun.

Some of the benefits participants receive during an *Art for Wellbeing* meeting are:

- Reaching a state of relaxation
- Practicing mindfulness
- Achieving meaningful insights
- Beginning on the path to healing
- Engaging socially (when attending a group session)

Initially, I was asked to help ignite Johanna's lost joy in filmmaking production and in screenwriting in particular. Johanna, a bright woman in her mid-30s, gained short film festival recognition during film school, yet the last time she wrote a screenplay was 10 years previously. Johanna's challenges included several health conditions and emotional challenges, including anxiety and depression. Her physical pain tended to debilitate her, typically on Mondays, and would then subside with prescribed medication.

Johanna believed that neither making films nor writing screenplays would sustain her financially. Right after graduation, she moved to Los Angeles with big dreams. Working 18+ hours on a film set as a production assistant disheartened her. There was no personal time for making her creative work, and she missed her friends and family on the East Coast. A friend who worked in the user experience (UX) design field helped her gain employment in New York City. Over time, Johanna climbed the professional ladder and had enjoyed the benefits of a management position in the same company for the past eight years. Her creativity was devoted to work-related projects that supported a comfortable lifestyle.

"I've never worked with a creativity coach before but I've had a therapist since my early teens," Johanna shared. "I need a lot of time to take in new information," she continued. I explained that coaching doesn't look at the past but that together in a partnership in which she would be held accountable we would seek to resolve present issues to enhance the quality of her life. We initially agreed to a six-month contract and arranged a once-a-month coaching session, with unlimited email and text communication in between sessions.

First, we looked into Johanna's lifestyle and examined what sort of an upgrade she desired to see. Screenplay writing was not a priority at the moment, Johanna made clear to me. She asked for support with dating and for approaching new career opportunities. I reviewed Johanna's resume, provided feedback and resources to improve it, and held close communication with her when she started to interview for new positions.

In regards to meeting men, we worked on her hesitation to create an online dating profile; I guided Johanna in that regard and invited her to keep an open mind. During one session, I volunteered my expertise in photography and took fresh pictures for Johanna for her dating profile. These came in handy and boosted her confidence. Soon, with motivation and encouragement, Johanna started to go out on dates and was happy for a short while.

Whenever Johanna faced pressure-filled deadlines at work, she shut off all communication channels and withdrew. That appeared to be her main coping mechanism with regard to stress. In addition, Johanna became devitalized usually during weekends, which is a time of rejuvenation for most. To manage to make it to work on Mondays, she increased her medication, which carried its own side effects. As we started to break down her day-to-day routine, I sensed that she was indulging in a lot of drinking, which alarmed me. I suspected that excessive alcohol intake was compromising her health.

"But I love drinking," Johanna said. She looked at me in disbelief. "I can stop at any time," she announced confidently. In response, I provided her with resources that described the signs of addiction to alcohol and alcohol's effects on the body. I designed a useful visual aid that included a plan for distracting herself from alcohol and dealing with the effects of alcohol withdrawal. I asked Johanna to place my visual reminder somewhere visible, hoping that she might actually use it. Johanna seemed to appreciate my gesture because she explained it was easier for her to comprehend visual diagrams than text. From then on, I continued creating visual aids during our sessions.

When I checked in on her drinking a few weeks later, Johanna explained that she had refrained from it for only a week. It was then, around the end of our fourth month working together, that I realized we were marching two steps forward and one step backward. I had witnessed Johanna's reoccurring physical pain. Johanna faced real stress from her managerial responsibilities and the added chemical stress from drinking. I decided to be pragmatic and challenge her in conversation. I shared that she could continue doing the same things over and over again as she did before or truly be open to work with me and try something new. That talk seemed beneficial and seemed to change and deepen our relationship.

As we continued our meetings together, I introduced Johanna to some simple deep-breathing techniques for relaxation, demonstrated how to meditate in easy steps, and shared visualization exercises that promote body healing. We discussed the importance of being proactive with using food as medicine to help prevent disease and alleviate anxiety and depression. I reminded her of the benefits of exercising and of stretching.

I explained complementary practices that use natural means to assist the body in healing, practices such as aromatherapy, traditional Chinese medicine, and herbs. In addition, we delved into the benefits of daily juicing and in particular using celery and an anti-inflammatory diet based on plants, with the recommendation to sparingly use organic fish and meat.

Before the end of our six-month contract, Johanna decided that we should continue working together. She indicated that she found coaching beneficial. At the following consultation, we looked into identifying, understanding, and expressing Johanna's feelings and emotions. We also looked at Johanna's thought patterns with a focus on reversing distorted thinking. Our work together required patience, understanding, and repetition of integrative concepts and wellness guidelines.

Around the seventh month mark, Johanna started to become more aware of her own power and her responsibility for taking care of her life. "I get it," she said, "there is much more to try than just drugs." We are still under contract, and it is wonderful to glimpse the joy in Johanna's eyes every time we meet in downtown Manhattan for a session. She is both calmer and more hopeful and knows that she can have my support whenever she needs it.

Johanna and I have not addressed her screenwriting yet, but I'm sure that we will. I think it makes sense to include a case study like this one in a collection of creativity coaching case studies because often the work that we do with creative clients is getting them ready to create, that is, setting the stage for their forthcoming creative efforts. If that's what's needed, then that's the work I need to do, when I'm qualified and able to do it. A lot of creativity coaching is not about "write your screenplay" but about "get yourself in position to write your screenplay."

Learning Points

1. A coach can help you a lot but you must own your part of the process. Go beyond any DSM diagnosis and surrender to the possibility of improvement. You may not achieve any immediate results, but if you trust yourself and the process you undertake, real improvement is possible.
2. Different clients have different needs in creativity coaching, and they learn what they need to know at their own paces. Neither coach nor client should feel too discouraged if it takes a little time for progress to be seen. In general, there will be noticeable results by the end of three months of working together. But patience is needed, from coach and client alike.
3. There is a balancing act in the unknown when deciphering anything new. Clients may well feel somewhat uncomfortable working to rid of long-held beliefs and ways of being. However, the reward of achieving one's full potential is a tremendous one. I am hopeful that Johanna will master the essential habits that help her body regenerate naturally as she releases the outdated paradigm that only synthetic drugs are the cure to pain and maybe finally gets back to her screenwriting.

Self-Coaching Questions

1. What are your own needs and motivations? Can you identify them?
2. As a coach, if you disagree with your client's values, choices, or habits, can you still accept her as a person?

3. As a coach, are you able to challenge your client if you believe that her behavior is hindering her?

About Nefeli Soteriou

Nefeli Soteriou helps unique individuals to move to the totality of possibilities in life, creativity, and wellbeing. She loves nature, exercise, and self-expression through art, adores animals, is interested in integrative medicine, produces indie narrative films and photography projects, holds an M.F.A in Film and Media Arts, and is a Creativity Coach and a NYS Holistic Wellness Counselor, with a background in teaching music, visual art, healthy cooking and interpersonal communication to all ages, from 5-89 years old. If you'd like to learn more about Nefelis's work as a coach and to contact her directly, visit: www.nefelisoteriou.com

Testimonials: www.nefelisoteriou.com/testimonials
Email: www.nefelisoteriou.com/contact-us
Bilingual service: Greek and English proficiency

Out of the Woods   **11**

A Talented Artist Returns to the Marketplace

Sheryl Garratt

"I don't think you'll be able to help me," Claire says when we first meet. She looks tired, anxious, fiddling nervously with her hair while she speaks. "But I have to try something because I can't go on like this."

A talented artist, Claire lives in the British countryside and makes work inspired by its wildlife and trees. When we met, she was selling her limited edition prints via a gallery in the small market town where she lived, at a rate of about one a month. The profit on each print was fairly low, however, and she was struggling to make ends meet, working part time in the gallery and waitressing at night to get by. The gallery owner had encouraged her to find other outlets and even offered her contacts to follow up on, but she hadn't done this, saying she simply hadn't been able to find the time.

Her last solo show at the gallery sold very well, but the owner hadn't offered her another one in the two years since, something she found upsetting. She considered him a friend, but her resentment was starting to affect that. "I feel angry," she admitted. "And taken for granted. I don't see why I'm always overlooked."

After a couple of sessions, we found two main challenges. Her work is beautifully thought-out, with fascinating stories and solid historical research behind them. But she wasn't telling these stories. On her website, the work was presented with little more than captions, her biographical information was dry as sand, and there was no information about how the works were made or the innovative techniques she was using.

We worked on really telling the stories on the website. Each series now has its own section, explaining the inspiration and research behind them, as well as giving technical information on how they were made. Photographs of her working in her studio and showing the work hanging in homes, bars, and restaurants give further information. She also added the measurements to show how large the pieces are. The next step will be adding a shop to sell directly online—one set of images would make great t-shirts, for instance.

Her bio is now sparky and interesting, and she has started using Twitter to show new work, to show work in progress, and to announce when pieces have sold. She is also creating more of a sense of urgency by counting down the number of prints remaining in each edition. "Edition of ten. Two remaining" tells potential buyers the work won't be available forever, especially when a couple in the series are now captioned, "Edition of ten. All sold."

We also practiced explaining the work and the processes and stories behind it to prospective buyers and dealers until she had a short, captivating introduction to share at networking events such as art openings and a longer but still clear and concise description for those showing real interest.

Then there was her attitude toward the gallery owner, which felt a little like Cinderella waiting for a fairy godmother to arrive and magically arrange for her to go the ball.

"Have you ever actually *asked* him for another show?" I wondered.

"No," she admitted. "But he knows I'm struggling, so he must know what it would mean to me."

"Must he?"

"Well . . . yes. Probably."

"So, there's a chance he doesn't know? That he can't actually read your mind?"

Claire laughed. "I suppose there is."

"So how would it feel to ask him directly?"

During this session, we rehearsed what she wanted to say, but at our next two sessions, she admitted she had been unable to find the right moment to broach the subject. She was worried what would happen if he turned her down.

"What's the worst that *could* happen?" I ask.

"He could sack me, stop selling my work altogether, I wouldn't be able to pay my rent, and I'd end up on the street."

"Really? You couldn't find any work at all to replace that two days of income?"

"Well, only more waitressing, immediately." She paused. "And there are probably other shops where I could find work. Or a temp agency."

"So that's the worst that could happen. How likely are you to be sacked, just for asking for a show?"

There was a silence. "Not very," she then said, smiling. "Really, the worst that could happen is, things would be a bit awkward between us, for a while."

"And what's the worst that could happen if you *don't* ask?"

She was thoughtful. "I think that's already happening. I'm angry, resentful. I'm even getting snappy with some of the other artists he represents. I'm not selling enough of my work. In fact, I'm on the verge of giving up making work at all."

Soon after, she took the plunge and asked. She didn't need the arguments she'd practiced; the gallery owner immediately said yes. He hadn't offered before, he explained, because she was constantly saying how tired she was and how little time she had, and he'd assumed it would be too much pressure to make so much new work.

The show is scheduled in four months' time. I suggested Claire use this as a reason to contact shops and galleries in other rural towns: she could show them the new work, invite them to her opening, and point them towards the revamped website. Having a clear story to tell and a deadline to work toward has given her incentive to do this, and she has now made these calls a regular part of her week. She has proved very resilient in the face of rejection. "My work isn't for everybody," she says, with a shrug. But her confidence has grown as others have responded favorably to her calls.

One small gallery asked her to bring in some work. After seeing it, they took it immediately. This new outlet has sold three pieces so far, encouraging Claire to increase her prices. Others have shown genuine interest and either committed to come to the show or made appointments to meet. Claire has also been contacted by a gallery that is 300 miles away. The gallery owner saw her work on Twitter, and she is developing ideas that might be more suitable for this new, more urban setting.

She has looked closely at her monthly budget and worked out that five galleries, each selling a print a month, would allow her to cut her waitressing hours dramatically. Ten outlets would give her real stability, enabling her to quit working in the evenings altogether.

When she gets to this point, we'll work on a plan to get media coverage and start contacting more prestigious city galleries. Claire now has a plan. She is excited about her work again and feels energized and full of hope for the future.

Learning Points

1. What helped Claire place her work in more galleries was getting clarity about the story she wanted to tell. Whether you're making an album, directing a film, promoting a book, or making any kind

of creative work to show to an audience, this is crucial. What is your story? What is interesting about you and your work? Often, we're so close to our processes and our projects that we are unable to see what is exciting. So, ask friends. Try telling the story behind your work in different ways and test the responses. And craft a captivating introduction, a couple of sentences to really describe what you do vividly. "I'm a writer" is one thing. "I'm working on a series of crime novels featuring a kick-ass, super-smart female detective with an unfortunate taste in men but a really great wardrobe" is more memorable, no?

2. The Internet and social media enable us to communicate with the world and share what we are doing cheaply and easily. Communicate regularly, put yourself out there, and you'll also start getting feedback and building new contacts in return. How could you use it to promote your work?

3. Accountability: Claire said she only finally asked for a solo show because she couldn't tell me she'd avoided it a third time. If you want to follow through on a difficult task, it helps to have someone to report back to, to hold you to it—and to praise you when it's done. This could be a coach, colleagues, or friends.

Self-Coaching Questions

1. Do you have a plan? Having a plan, realizing how little it would take to replace her waitressing income with income from her art, was another incentive for Claire to pick up the phone and sell. If you are struggling, it's good to know your bottom line: how much money do you really need to survive if you cut back on absolutely all unnecessary spending? It may be less than you imagine. And how much would you need to earn to feel secure, to be able to enjoy a slightly better standard of living, with a few treats and luxuries? What would it take to get to the first figure and then the second? Once you've got there, start putting a percentage of your earnings aside, building up a savings cushion for added security. Also put a percentage away to invest in your creativity. This is money to spend, guilt free, on equipment, travel, training, help with bookkeeping, chores, admin—whatever you need to grow as an artist.

2. Risk can be scary. Ask yourself: what's the worst that could happen? Then examine how likely that really is and what you would do if your worst-case scenario unfolds. But then also ask: what's the worst that could happen if I *don't* take this risk? Fear often stops us from performing that new music, showing radical new work, pressing publish on that blog post. But even if we fail, we'll have learned from it. Some rejection is surely better than making work that is never seen at all?

3. Have you created appropriate deadlines? Having a deadline and a concrete reason for calling helped Claire pick up the phone and talk to other galleries. Create urgency, if you have to. Set a date to release a song, book a hall for a show, organize a reading of your work. Then use it to motivate yourself.

About Sheryl Garratt

Sheryl Garratt has earned her living as a writer for many years and now helps musicians, writers, designers, artists, and other creatives and solopreneurs tell their stories well, overcome the blocks preventing them from doing their best work, and prepare for their next big, bold projects. She lives on the English coast, works regularly in London, and meets with clients worldwide via phone or Zoom. She can be found online at www.thecreativelife.net.

How Samson Grew His Hair Back

A Photographer Prevails

Rahti Gorfien

Nick's physical complaints only made his already difficult situation worse. Symptoms of fibromyalgia include widespread pain in the muscles and bones, sleep disorders, depression, and fatigue. According to the National Fibromyalgia Association, for every eight women who are diagnosed with this debilitating condition, one man is diagnosed. My client Nick was the rare and unfortunate representative of that statistic.

Men with these complaints are often labeled as 'wimpy,' 'lazy,' 'whiny,' and 'weak.' Experts admit that because of these negative characterizations, many men go misdiagnosed or nondiagnosed. Suffice it to say, these negative characterizations did nothing for Nick's self-esteem, which already suffered because of his lack of financial self-sufficiency at the age of 38 and the cultural black-and-white thinking he'd bought into regarding what constitutes a successful artist in this culture.

He wasn't making a living at his photography, he wasn't consistently creating, and he wasn't experiencing widespread recognition for his work. This state of affairs further defined him as a failure in his own eyes. To make matters worse, Nick came from a legacy of suicide. His father had taken his own life when Nick was a teenager, in no small part I imagine for reasons related to congenital, perhaps undiagnosed and untreated conditions he'd passed on to his son.

When he came to me, Nick was at a real low point. He hadn't picked up his camera in a year. "I have a cloud over my head that needs to be lifted," he told me during our consultation. "I can't live like this any longer." Now, when a coach hears something like "I can't live like this any longer" coming from a prospective client with a family history of suicide, which he was very forth-coming about, alarm bells go off big time. My first internal dialogue went something like this: "You've got no business taking this fellow's money. Refer him to a shrink immediately."

Happily, when I asked, it turned out that he was already in treatment with a therapist. "I think we could work together," I told him. The first order of business would be to reignite his belief in his own self-determination and his ability to make meaning of his existence. To my mind, the shifts that needed to occur in coaching had to do with this lack of meaning or the 'why' of his continued existence, especially in relation to his creative work.

This is why he'd called me, after all, having googled "creative coach in Brooklyn." We agreed that the goal of our relationship was to remedy that felt lack of meaning. Therapy and medication would be part of our overall strategy, at least for a while, enabling him to make the internal shifts required to get out of inertia and back into the field with his camera.

And so, with his agreement to stay in treatment and with the goal of our work together being to unleash his productivity and start marketing his work, we met via videoconference three times a month. Originally, he'd wanted to work in person, which is why he sought out someone local, but one sub-way ride and one face-to-face meeting left him feeling drained for the rest of the day, so we agreed that given his physical and energetic challenges, it was worth giving virtual sessions a try.

As is my usual practice prior to an initial session, I asked Nick to fill out a Life Wheel. This simple assessment is a pie chart divided into 10 slices, each one corresponding to a different aspect of life. It is completed by drawing a line across each slice in relation to a scale of 1 to 10, 10 being closest to the periphery of the circle and 1 being closest to its center. As such, 10 equals perfection, and 1 is basically rock bottom.

Here's what Nick's Life Wheel pie looked like when we started:

Spiritual—6
Career—2
Finances—5
Environment—5
Family—5
Significant Other / Romance—7
Friends / Community—3
Personal Development / Education—5
Health and Fitness—2
Fun / Recreation / Self-Care—2

We talked about how the different areas of his life correlated with one another and affected each other. He had a decent foundation across the board survival-wise: a stable and fairly ordered living environment and sufficient finances, thanks in part to ungrudging support from his family and a partner who loved him. He had a desire to live, evidenced by his willingness to use his resources in support of his personal development. In terms of spirituality, he had found his way to Buddhist meditation, which helped him deal with his symptoms and kept him from 'going off the deep end.'

As it turned out, Nick's spiritual orientation as a Buddhist was very helpful in our work and served as a powerful point of reference to which we returned again and again. Initially, he needed support with the basics, such as being able to count on himself to get out of bed in the morning without an external motivation such as getting to his job as a substitute teacher. Without that, the morning depression and physical pain he would experience could be over-whelming enough to keep him in bed until the late afternoon. So, we took a look at his capacity to overcome his challenges for others but not for himself.

"Why is that, do you think?" I asked.

"I don't know."

We sat in silence for a while, a couple of miles across Prospect Park from each other in front of our respective screens one cloudy Wednesday after-noon. Nick stared at his keyboard.

"I don't know" is usually a client's first answer. It's difficult, but I've learned to sit with some very long pauses during sessions following that response.

"I guess if I'm not doing something for somebody else, then it doesn't mat-ter enough for me to deal with getting out of bed," he finally said.

"What do you mean by 'matter'?"

"You know . . . make any difference."

"What makes something make a difference?"

"I don't know. Maybe nothing does."

"I don't think you believe that. If you did, you wouldn't get up for any-body."

Nick paused. I could see his eyes getting watery.

"It's just . . . everything is so damned hard."

"Yeah. It is. But even though it's damned hard, when you feel you have to, you get stuff done. If nothing matters, then maybe you decide what does, and when you believe something matters, you rise to the occasion."

"Yeah. Like not losing my job and being totally dependent on my girlfriend and family."

"Exactly. So why does your photography matter?"

"Maybe it doesn't."

"Well, if you were to decide that it did, what would *make* it matter?"

"Well . . . it's my way of seeing things. And when I'm doing it, it just feels like it's "where I belong.'

"How do you feel physically while you're taking pictures and working with the images?"

"Nothing hurts."

"Sounds like good medicine. Like breathing or eating."

"Yeah."

"Breathing and eating matter, wouldn't you say?"

Nick smiled. We were on our way.

That week, Nick shot a roll of Polaroid Time Zero film with an expiration date of 1981 that came in a camera he'd bought as a collectible. He didn't believe that it was possible for integral film to last that long without the chemicals drying out, but something made him give it a try. I don't usually look at clients' work, but sometimes they'll scan and email it to me without asking. Nick's images were beautiful, abstract, and haunting . . . and they would not have existed without this man's unique vision and intimate knowledge of pain and despair. Moreover, the work existed despite that pain and despair.

Nick found it within himself to keep going by seeking and accepting proper support. It was by no means a straight trajectory from there to exhibiting and selling his work, but he succeeded in doing so eventually by learning how to keep returning to his *why*.

Learning Points

1. It's important to tend to your own unique needs by being open to any modality that can lend support. After all, there is no shame in using a bronchial dilator if you have asthma.
2. Even when life is hard, we prevail when we believe that we must. And we must when we believe that it matters to do so.
3. Whether what you create matters or doesn't matter is not an objective truth. Your creative work matters once you decide that it does. This can sometimes be an impossible decision to make on one's own, through a lens of pain and despair, without help. And it may not be a decision that can be made all at once.

Self-Coaching Questions

1. What do you need to do to feel ready to face the day? Meditate? Listen to inspirational podcasts? Make the bed?
2. What is non-negotiable in your life, regardless of how you feel? Why is that non-negotiable?
3. What would it be like to decide that creating was non-negotiable, and *why* might you make that decision?

About Rahti Gorfien

As the founder of Creative Calling Coaching, Rahti Gorfien is a professionally certified career, ADHD, and creativity coach who has been helping her clients profit from their passion for over 15 years. She was recently recognized as one of the top 15 life coaches in New York City by Expertise.com. Specializing in work with artists and entrepreneurs who struggle with ADHD or chronic physical conditions, Gorfien assists her clients in creating unique ways to move their art, businesses, and lives forward through emphasis on prioritization, self-structuring, and mindfulness.

Website: https://creativecallingcoaching.com/faq/
Facebook: https://bit.ly/2UkfMdm
Instagram: @coachrahti
Twitter: @Rahti

When Pain Strikes   **13**

Building a New Life After a Divorce

Rosa Phoenix

"We were in this *together*," Benny said ruefully. "We made vows to stick together *for life*." His voice raised to a higher pitch, his lower lip trembled, and his face reddened. Tears welled in his eyes, but stubbornly, they did not fall.

He sat for a moment in silence. When he spoke again it was so quiet, it was almost a whisper.

"How can I do this by myself?"

Days after his 50th birthday, Benny's wife of 25 years had dropped a bombshell on him—she was divorcing him and moving back to Philadelphia.

Benny was an industrial designer, but for the better part of the past decade, he longed to make a dramatic change in his career and environment. He'd become tired with the way technology had made his work monotonous, spending countless hours in front of his computer, endlessly tweaking CAD drawings. He longed to work with his hands and get dirty, to honor the Earth and promote sustainable ways of living, and to focus on earth-based architecture.

To prepare for this shift, he had gone to various workshops to learn how to build cob houses and had toured ancient dwellings to study and take notes for something he would eventually design and build himself. He dreamed of building an ecological retreat center, hosting people, and teaching workshops about earth-based building and sustainable design.

A year prior to his wife announcing her plans to leave him, they had taken a winter vacation to the desert town of Cave Creek, Arizona, and fell in love with the spare and haunting desert landscape. The environment had awoken in them a longing they had felt for years, to live a simple life, being part of and close to nature. Their journey to Arizona had felt like a magical homecoming. They decided to move there.

They found their ideal building site and purchased the parcel, and Benny began excitedly drawing up the plans. The plot of land was off a primitive dirt road, with a dry wash running through it, tall saguaro cacti, scrubby sagebrush, and an expansive view of a distant, craggy mountain range. Best of all, a mineral spring trickled out of a clutch of rocks, more valuable than gold in the desert.

The concept was to slowly build an Earthship (a sustainable, energy-generating home fashioned out of recycled materials) and a couple of simple cob buildings constructed of clay and straw. Eventually, they'd dig a pool for the mineral spring and use the water to irrigate organic gardens. Over time, a small eco-village would grow. Benny's wife was enthusiastic about the plans, too, or so Benny thought.

Benny arranged to work remotely, as did his wife. They came out to Arizona and contracted the groundwork—digging a foundation for the main house, laying the lines for infrastructure—while Benny continued with his building designs from a little mobile home on the land.

Then the disaster struck. Benny's wife had gone back to Philadelphia to take care of some family business. She realized she didn't want to leave her life in Philadelphia. "I've had a change of heart," she texted him. She never came back.

Here Benny was, alone for the first time in his life, away from everyone and everything he knew. He had no wife or home to go back to in Philadelphia anymore.

"I'm stuck," Benny said when he contacted me, seeking support for his building project. "I can't go back, but I can't move forward, either. Whenever I try to do building work, pain takes over, and I literally can't move."

Since Benny's wife left, he started having debilitating back pain and migraines. He had been to see doctors and specialists. He was applying ice and heat. The specialists were recommending spinal fusion, but he didn't want to do that. He was receiving chiropractic and acupuncture treatments that helped him temporarily. He hadn't made progress on the property for weeks.

"I'm spineless, and I'm out of my mind, literally" said Benny with a humorless laugh. "I feel helpless. I feel weak, and it disgusts me."

He felt he had something to prove to his ex-wife. That he could go ahead alone. That he didn't need her. That he was strong and capable. He was angry that his body was betraying him.

After assessing whether Benny truly wanted to continue with the building project (he did), I invited Benny to look more carefully at the pain. "Can you describe the painful episodes: what are the physical sensations, and are they associated with any particular thoughts, feelings, or actions?" I inquired.

He agreed to monitor his feelings over the next couple of weeks and report back to me.

"I got an email about the divorce, and it triggered me," said Benny in our next session. "I went outside to work on the building. Then I started thinking about how much longer it will take for me to do this without any help and without much money because it's all going away with the divorce. I started feeling these hot, electric zinging sensations rushing up my spine, so intense I almost fell down. My heart started pounding really fast, I felt heat swelling in my throat, and my face broke out into a sweat like I ate chili peppers. Then I got a migraine that felt like my head was splitting, and I had to go inside and lie down for a couple hours. My day was shot."

"The body sends us messages," I said. "What message are you getting from this?"

Benny thought for a few moments. "Danger," he said. "'Anger leads to danger' is what comes to my mind."

"Right, anger leads to danger. And anger is also a natural, normal emotion that needs to be felt, before you can let it go, and get out of danger. You've done a wonderful job with allowing yourself to feel the feelings fully. Now let's work on ways to release them."

We discussed the nature of anger as a hot energy and how, just as a machine can become overheated, the body can also shut down.

"The next time you experience 'anger leading to danger,'" I said, "I want you to visualize that energy as a hot blazing cloud moving up and out through the crown of your head, escaping and blowing up and out to the sky, like smoke releasing through a chimney stack."

Benny agreed to try. The next time, after feeling the electric rush of heat, he felt a tingling sensation in the crown of his head and a few inches above followed by lightheaded dizziness and loss of equilibrium that lasted for several minutes. He still got back pain and a migraine, but it wasn't as severe as before.

Next, we worked on instilling some calming, grounding practices to maintain a sense of stability.

Benny started running as a way to "burn it off." He began running every morning and evening. After "burning it off," he took an ice-cold shower and visualized the water cooling and cleansing him. This became his self-care practice.

I wanted to balance the upward rushing energy of Benny's anger with grounding and stabilizing energy, so I recorded a guided meditation for him to listen to that focused on rooting deep into the life energy of the Earth and breathing it in deeply.

Benny reconnected with his reason for wanting to work in sustainability and his desire to give back what he had been given.

He began to release pain and anger more quickly. "It's like the desert storms here," he said. "Quickly moving through with a lot of drama and then gone in a flash."

Over time, Benny began to feel more grounded, stable, and supported. He had fewer painful episodes and migraines. He didn't get as triggered. His passion for his project renewed, and he was able to get back to work.

When pain had become less of an issue for him, I said, "I think you have a wonderful opportunity with your project. You're in a new environment, building your dream, and at the same time, you're rebuilding your life."

"That's true," said Benny. "I've been focused on feeling angry and wronged and feeling sorry for myself for what I lost. But I am building my dream as well, and I'm lucky to do so."

Using the metaphor of building his eco-retreat and rebuilding his life, I asked Benny to list both his personal needs and his needs for his building project, and then we brainstormed areas of overlap, ways that he could simultaneously get his needs met in both areas.

Through writing, Benny determined that he needed to love and nurture others, connect with community, and get help with the building process. Based on this exercise, Benny invited friends to come out and spend time with him and help on the property. He also registered with a network that connects volunteers with ecologically friendly projects.

Hosting visitors allowed Benny to teach and share his passion with others throughout the building process, while his visitors and volunteers helped with the work. Benny saw his dream becoming manifested quickly, not as he expected but in a way that brought him a sense of fulfillment and excitement.

Learning Points

1. Your body sends messages in the form of physical sensations. "Listen" to these messages by noticing when they arise and any thoughts or feelings that are associated with them.
2. When you are in a state of overwhelm, find ways to feel, direct, and release the energy. Then use grounding activities and visualizations or meditations to bring yourself back to balance.

3. Look for opportunities to fulfill your personal needs while also working on your creative project.

Self-Coaching Questions

1. What thoughts or emotions aggravate painful or uncomfortable sensations for you?
2. What are some ways you can fulfill your needs for love and community, outside of your primary relationship?
3. What might you choose as a metaphor for what you are creating in your project, a metaphor that can also serve for what you want to create in your personal life?

About Rosa Phoenix

Rosa Phoenix is a visual artist, art teacher, and creativity coach. She guides people on a transformative journey to discover their own creative potential and the healing powers of the creative process. Her approach is intuitive and mindfulness-based, frequently blending visual art activities with other art forms such as writing and music, and body-centered practices such as yoga, breath work, and gentle movement. She offers classes, workshops, retreat facilitation, and one-on-one coaching. She is based in the United States. To learn more, please visit www.rosaphoenix.com.

Foiling Perfectionism **14**

The Magic of Lowered Expectations

Jill Badonsky

I present to you Helen, a woman in her 70s who achieved a vast amount of fame earlier in life and came to me for my help to write her memoir. Although famous, she struggled with common obstacles many of us encounter on our way to create.

Helen had volumes of journals filled with her rise to fame, loss, abuse, and transcendence she experienced in her life; the task of distilling them into a memoir confounded her to the point of paralysis. She was stopped by fear and expectations: having no idea where to begin to write, feeling overwhelmed with the amount of accumulated material, and fearing that at her age, this memoir may never happen. As a world traveler, she gave presentations plus took care of her renowned husband, so little time was left for concentrated writing.

There was clear frustration in her voice when she described tethering herself to the goal of writing a best-selling masterpiece despite the high demands on her time but also because much of her energy went to meeting the needs of her internationally recognized husband. Her need to operate far above the average made it clear that perfectionism had her in its insidious grip.

Perfectionism can be considered glorified self-sabotage—its demand on us is oppressive, and we often choose avoidance in the face of ridiculously high-pressured intentions we aren't even aware we've set for ourselves. Not meeting these expectations can leave us disappointed, which is another way to dampen our self-expression.

Helen's dedication to her husband's work left little acknowledgement for her own remarkable story. It was important to give her as much uninterrupted time to share her fantastic story as possible.

Creative people need to be heard. When they are required to put their stories on a back burner for other responsibilities, resentment can further sap energy needed to take steps toward expression. A bonding process began that evolved into the type of coach–client relationship needed to sustain encouragement for Helen with reinforcement for habits of thought needed for her to stay true to her voice.

If they don't have an understanding of the dynamics caused by fears and expectations, clients have no move to counter or neutralize the obstacles, so they feel alone.

I asked Helen to describe what she had in mind for the memoir. Her answer: "A spell-binding, enchanting, provocative, truthful, beguiling work where the readers felt loved as they read it."

I repeated her words back to her and noted, "Those are beautiful words," and added, "but do you think your expectations at the beginning might be putting an unduly amount of pressure on you?" She agreed.

I find it vital to ask creative people questions rather than tell them my ideas and theories. Respect prevents the rebellion that results from being told what to do or giving them a lecture.

"It's totally understandable that you would feel overwhelmed. I would too. That is a LOT of material to distill! Many writers feel overwhelmed at this stage. You're not alone. You have an incredible story to share, and often we resort to avoidance when we put so much pressure on ourselves. Does that make sense?"

That question turned a lecture into a considerate check-in.

This normalized her challenges. Normalizing a common reaction to creative expression can relax us enough to move us into action. It's freeing to feel we are experiencing the same thing as others on a path instead of thinking we are suffering a weakness that is uniquely ours. Helen expressed a great sense of relief when I normalized her situation.

Helen also worried that she was losing her ability to write by not making time for it. When I hear a client tell me they cannot find the time, are feeling pressure, or are losing their courage to start, the Kaizen-Muse Creativity Coaching (KMCC) tools I use are:

1. A guided relaxation moves them from a pressured mental chaos of "should" and comparisons to intuition and clarity.
2. Move the client into action DURING the session.
3. Lower the pressure of unreasonable expectations.

Setting aside time during the coaching call happens when clients announce that they haven't made progress in their pursuits. Involving them in experiences during the call not only makes the session more valuable, but it also instantly breaks resistance to BEGIN. Just a few minutes engaged in writing during the call can lead to a momentum that will allow them to continue after the call is over. If instead I were to fill a session with more pressure to do activities outside the session, that can just add to feelings of overwhelm and ultimately to the abandonment of coaching.

I asked Helen if she would be willing to do some writing during the session, which predictably triggered her resistance. Avoidance can be a comfortable habit for some people.

"What if we do a quick five-minute writing exercise just for fun and purposely shoot for a terribly bad first draft?"

This intrigued her. She relaxed and agreed. A guided relaxation further relaxed her. Due to being in charge of workshops, organizing travel and attending to her partner's needs, this left little time for her own restoration. Helen was thrilled to focus on herself.

I guided her through a simple relaxation that called upon her creative resources. It reminded her that even when she's not making time for her creativity, it's always there; it gave her permission to trust that when she's ready, the work will happen; and it invited her to let the words flow on the page however they wanted.

We took turns coming up with words prior to beginning the writing. We took five minutes to weave those words into an "awful piece of writing." I informed her I was holding the space for her to do this.

When the five minutes were up, I asked if she wanted to share anything about the experience. She proceeded to read out loud a beautiful prose piece, gracefully engineered with spiritual brilliance. I asked her how she felt about it, and she started crying, relieved that she could still write, inspired to write more. She seemed in awe that shooting for awful writing could result in something she loved. The lowering of expectations can relax us enough for our true selves to emerge.

Close to the session's end, I asked Helen what the most helpful part of the session was for her. She identified the guided relaxation, especially the part about trusting that her creativity would always be there, and the actual writing.

I told her I was going to make some suggestions and asked her to let me know which sounded good to her.

1. I suggested that she get a little "reminder journal" and that she put in it a few reminders from our session: The creativity is always there, I can relax

my standards and still write things I love, and I can ask myself what it would feel like to trust that this work will be done.

2. I suggested that we meet for "parallel universe time" when we could both write the way we did in the session, separate from our next coaching call.

3. I suggested that she spend just five minutes with one of her journals, rereading what she'd written and taking notes about what might be included in her memoir, not worrying about anything other than that. At the end of five minutes, she could continue if she was caught up in the momentum. The experience of successfully writing for five minutes would give her a sense of accomplishment that would encourage her to write more. Next, she could ask herself what tiny step intuitively felt like the next.

She chose all of the suggestions. I encouraged her to start with just five minutes of revisiting her work. This excited her, and she ended up reading pieces to me on our next calls.

Through our work, Helen found that sharing her experience in blogs and in social media met her need to get her story out and was met with a bigger response than she expected. We continued working together during sessions, generating more and more organization and clarity, keeping the expectations kind, and continuing the reminder that trust works better than fear.

Learning Points

1. Lowering our expectations gets us started. It relaxes us and often results in better work than unreasonable expectations. If you feel avoidance or resistance, keep breaking down your expectations into smaller parts until it's easy and enticing to begin. Take five minutes to take a small step toward what you want to do. A question can count as a small step.

2. Relax; it's normal to feel fear or resistance. Any challenge you are experiencing is a normal part of the process. You're not alone.

3. Team up with a friend. The buddy system is one of the most effective ways to get to our work. You can simply call each other, set an intention, and hold the space from 15 minutes to an hour. I do this at least once a week with a friend; we stay on the phone but are quietly writing on our own work.

Self-Coaching Questions

1. How would it feel to lower my expectations of my work just a bit to make it easier to begin? What tiny step can I begin with?
2. What's worked for me in the past? Can I do that again?
3. How can I make this easier? How can I make it fun?

About Jill Badonsky

Jill Badonsky, MEd, is the author and illustrator of three books on the creative process, including *The Muse Is In: An Owner's Manual to Your Creativity*. She is founder and director of Kaizen-Muse Creativity Coaching Certification training and has been training creativity coaches since 2004. She posts a wacky creativity prompt every day on Facebook. Visit her website at www.kaizen muse.com.

How Confidence Breeds Creativity

15

A Retired Reporter Breaks Free From Self-Doubt

Halli Bourne

Patrick, a high-powered political reporter, never intended to retire. But his 71st birthday brought a string of unforeseen life events that shook his foundations like tremors before a big earthquake. First there were the piercing headaches. Then the heart murmur and bouts of insomnia. Then the heart attack he only narrowly survived. His doctors were clear: *retire or die . . . the stress is literally killing you.*

Having worked doggedly since he was a teenager, Patrick had no idea how to be retired. "Who am I now?" he kept asking himself. "What do I do with myself if I'm not working?" A sense of anxiety and emptiness clouded his idle days, so he determined to return to something familiar—writing.

When he called on me for creativity coaching, he'd been struggling to pen short fiction. He told me he felt plagued by self-doubt that kept him from the keyboard. When he did manage to sit down to write, he was overcome by critical inner voices telling him he didn't have any talent and that fiction writing was a foolish endeavor. He wanted help silencing these voices.

In our first session, I suggested a free-writing exercise to explore the "why" of his writing.

"Imagine your ideal reader," I told him. "What line of work are they in? What's going on in their life? How will reading your book make a difference? No detail is off limits. For the sake of doing something different, write with actual pen and paper without stopping for 15 minutes. Be willing to be a beginner and just see what happens."

In our next session, Patrick was surprised to find that many of the qualities of his "ideal reader" essentially described himself. When I suggested this to him, he forced a smile, as if to say he wanted to believe me but wasn't quite ready to.

Yet he was feeling encouraged, so he asked for help figuring out a topic for his first short story. He enthusiastically agreed when I suggested leading him through a visualization to help him access his imagination. He sat back and closed his eyes, as I told him to slow down and deepen his breath, to release all the tension he held in his body.

"See yourself in a field of endless possibility," I began. "There's a deep forest on the other side of the field, and you feel drawn it. As you get closer, you see an enormous, antique display cabinet. Each shelf holds objects you recognize . . . characters and dramas from your life that represent some topic you've been thinking of writing about. Keep an open and curious mind as you peer at the items in the cabinet. Pay special attention to the ones that catch your eye. What do they look like? What colors and shapes are they? How do they make you feel?"

After about a minute, Patrick's eyes were still closed but squinting. I could see his breath had gone quick and shallow in his chest. I asked him to take a deep breath and open his eyes.

"Tell me about the objects you saw," I prompted gently.

"Well, there was a replica of the White House . . . and I thought of writing about corruption in politics. And then there was a bobblehead doll of a guy in a tie, and I thought about how destructive big egos are. . . ."

"Was there any particular object that drew you more than the others?"

Patrick's face softened, and a smile played around his mouth. "Yeah, there was the inkwell and Shaeffer fountain pen my mom gave me for high school graduation. She always thought I'd be a 'great writer' someday."

"And when you think about great writing, what do you imagine?"

At this, a pall darkened his face. "I hear my father in my head, telling me I should be a lawyer like he was." Then, in an unbroken stream, Patrick recounted a devastating experience from early in his reporting career.

It was his first big break. He'd been flown to a remote island to investigate a stewing government scandal, but from the moment he stepped off the plane, he was beset by misadventures. His luggage was lost. His driver never showed at the airport. Scheduled interviews kept getting cancelled. Despite his best efforts, he returned to the bureau a week later with a bare sketch of the scandal. The story he cobbled together was a profound disappointment. The island's readership fumed, accusing him of being misrepresentative and offensively reductionist. His father's backhanded suggestion was to consider another career. All this criticism shook his confidence to the core; a deep, pernicious fear and self-doubt seeped into his bones and festered there.

"So here I am," he concluded in a resigned voice. "So many years have passed—and so has my father—and despite my long career as a reporter, I'm still obsessed about what people are going to think." His voice broke, and he bowed his head, trying to regain control of himself.

I attempted to hide my satisfied smile. We had arrived at the cause of his writer's block.

"Patrick, consider this," I urged. "If you didn't care what anyone else thought, what would you WANT to write about? What would get you excited to sit down at the keyboard?"

He lifted his shoulders up toward his ears, as though experimenting with the weight he'd been carrying, and dropped them down with an expansive sigh. "I'd write about all the changes I've just been through . . . about facing my own mortality and who I am now. But that's just my experience. Who else would want to?" He looked up at me, realization blossoming on his face. "Now I know why I couldn't figure out what to write," he murmured. "There are all these specters . . . naysayers reminding me of how I screwed up. I have to let all that go. I'll never write anything if I keep worrying about what people think."

With his obstacles clearly in focus, Patrick began strategically dissolving them. I taught him simple breathing and meditation techniques to help him shift from overthinking to creativity, and I showed him how to summon his newly inspired voice whenever he sat down to write. The more he practiced, the more he was able to calmly and objectively observe his inner critic before pivoting back to his imagination and his reason for writing. He began looking forward to his practices and ultimately felt more relaxed and enthusiastic when it was time to write.

One year later, he had completed his first piece of short fiction—a moving tale of impermanence, mortality, and the triumph of persistence. Through his art, Patrick found a way to give voice to his bottled-up years of experience and a new meaning to his retirement.

Learning Points

If you've ever felt paralyzed by what others think, consider the nature of criticism. Even though we often crave approval, it isn't always what's best for our work. Moreover, sometimes the critics have no idea what they're talking about. Constructive criticism can help us improve, and at other times it's best to step back and give yourself some credit. When you receive criticism—even if it's been internalized from long ago—remember to give yourself the benefit of the doubt and treat yourself with compassion. When you learn to do this at the first sign of self-doubt, your inner critic will lose its foothold, and you will empower yourself to free your own potential.

1. *Consider the source*—It's easy to criticize, and everyone's a critic. You will always have dissenters. There are some who say if you're not getting any criticism, you're not having an effect! Consider people's motivation and either put their feedback in a category you find helpful or let it go entirely. Remember that all feedback is delivered through a subjective filter and may simply be an opinion, a projection, or a competitive ploy. If *you* are the source of your criticism, get to know your emotional triggers and choose to release criticism you've internalized from your past. Treat yourself with compassionate attention and take care of your old wounds.

2. *Learn techniques to relax and focus*—Some social psychologists have claimed that fear of criticism and rejection relates to our tribal history, when our likeability and inclusion determined our survival. Even now, criticism can certainly *feel* like life or death. Take the time to learn techniques that will relax your body and calm your anxiety, such as visualization, meditation, and deep breathing. *Try this:* Close your eyes and "look" inside. Where do you notice physical tension? When your mind touches that tension, deepen your breath and imagine your energy filling that tension and expanding it, like air in a balloon.

3. *Give yourself permission to be wonderful and flawed*—When you are connected to what gives your life meaning and you understand that *all* of you (not just the bright and cheery parts) contributes to that meaning, you can allow criticism to flow naturally into the stream of your life. Stand at the center of your own life, sourcing your identity from who you truly are rather than someone else's version of you. Give up the need to measure yourself against false standards. Become skeptical of your inner critic and stay committed to excelling at being you.

Self-Coaching Questions

1. How is the fear of criticism holding you back?
2. What would you do if you *didn't* fear criticism?
3. How can you improve the ways you currently receive criticism?

About Halli Bourne

As a transition coach, Halli helps her clients transform change and loss into opportunities for self-knowledge and self-actualization. Working with seekers and creatives, she provides tools, teachings, and practices to infuse life with meaning and inspiration. She believes true happiness and a sense of purpose come from creating internal spaciousness, self-compassion, and authenticity.

Halli is a certified creativity coach, and she has been practicing and teaching yoga and meditation for the past 25 years while living a wild and precious life as a psychonaut, uncovering paths to physical and spiritual healing. She is a licensed (nonpracticing) massage therapist, certified craniosacral therapist, a reiki master, actor, director, poet, writer, musician, vocalist, songwriter, dancer, and visual artist. She has a BA in theatre arts.

The Ugly Sculpture That Wasn't

16

Jennifer Rediscovers Her Creative Identity

Sharon J. Burton

A note popped up one day on my Facebook messenger that intrigued me. A writer named Jennifer, who had participated with me in a Facebook group, sent a note about her interest in my creative services. We connected initially by email, and Jennifer shared that she wanted to launch a podcast, but after a few attempts, she felt frustrated and blocked. She asked me to help her overcome her anxiety regarding this new endeavor and move past the blocks she was experiencing.

During our first meeting via Zoom, Jennifer shared in detail about launching this new podcast that would focus on various topics about writing as a means for self-expression. Jennifer had recruited her first two guests and tried to record their interview multiple times, but some technical malfunction had happened, leaving her feeling devastated and like a failure. She began to question the entire podcast concept and seemed at a loss about how to move forward with the process.

Since I have produced podcasts off and on since 2007, I understood that technical difficulties are always a part of the game. Intuitively, I believed there was something behind her frustration that was beyond working with podcast technology and was curious about what her feeling like a failure was really about.

I decided that the best approach was to help her explore where the nucleus of her creative block might be coming from. I suspected that she could be falling into "imposter syndrome" when she questioned her identity as a creative person because of some early messaging. Imposter syndrome can often be traced to a negative comment or discouragement from someone a person deems important or significant in his or her life.

I asked Jennifer to talk about her past creative projects, particularly what she was proud of and why. She first shared about a simple drawing she did in elementary school and how her father was so impressed with it that he placed it on the refrigerator in their home for everyone to see.

However, as it often happens, through the conversation, another not so positive story appeared from her high school days. Jennifer had created a sculpture, which she has to this day, in response to an art teacher's assignment. She recalled that her teacher was very critical of the sculpture and embarrassed her in front of other students. The teacher declared that Jennifer could never be an artist because of her "lack of talent."

From that day forward, Jennifer stopped creating art for several years. When she felt the urge to create, she would do pottery or drawings but would never show them to anyone. Although she later embarked on a successful writing career, she had a belief based on the feedback of this one art teacher that she was not an artist or had any creativity at all.

I challenged her to see if deep inside whether this was a story that she truly believed. I suggested that she do the following to help her connect to the creative artist that she had lost:

1. Make a list of why you don't feel that you are a creative person. Look at the list and then write a counter list of positive affirmations that negate what you wrote. Example: "I am not an artist because I didn't go to art school." Affirmation: "I am an artist because I express myself creatively."

2. Take notice and journal some of the negative things people said about your art. Who are these people? What did they say? Think of what was happening at the time, the situation and your emotions. How would you address these people today? I suggested an exercise that Julia Cameron provided in her book, *The Artist's Way*, in which she challenges the reader to write a letter to the person who discouraged your creative efforts in the voice of who you were at the time that it happened, in support of yourself. Julia suggested mailing the letter to yourself.

3. Think about the people who you consider fans of your creativity. A quick way to get this information is to look at the people who wrote complimentary messages on Facebook to something you shared that you created (a program, a course, a workshop, and so on). Or think about what your father said about your drawing when you were a kid. How can you thank them or show your gratitude?

Jennifer completed the assignment and emailed her answers. Several stories came up for her regarding critics, including some family members. She also shared a photo of her sculpture that caused much of the pain in high school, a sculpture that was gorgeous. She came to our next Zoom meeting with a new level of excitement and optimism.

During our second session, she shared how the exercise opened her eyes about how she was viewing herself and that the positive reinforcement from others in her life who have been supportive of her endeavors provided new energy to move forward with her creativity. She also mentioned that she recently found the original drawing that her dad celebrated years ago.

The next assignment focused on a few more activities to help her move forward with reclaiming her creative identity, which included the following:

1. Find artwork from your childhood and place it in your writing space or studio so you can see it and be reminded of the positive reinforcement behind it.
2. With a new-found feeling of confidence, create a self-portrait of yourself as a creative person. It can look like you in human form or reflect colors, shapes, or textures that represent your creative spirit.
3. Type or write out all the affirmative statements from friends who commented on your Facebook posts and place them around your home as reminders of the support you have currently.

In between the second and third sessions, Jennifer emailed me a beautiful self-portrait that represented her creative self. She noted how good it felt to create this self-portrait using markers and paint. During our third session, she truly was glowing on the Zoom video conference. She discussed how she reviewed some of her past Facebook posts sharing her programs and writings and the beautiful, affirming words people shared with her about her work. Jennifer created several positive affirmations that she posted around her home as reminders of her creative talents. Her sculpture, once abandoned in the attic, was now front and center in her studio office. The artwork that her father praised now was framed and held a prominent place in her home as well.

As a result of our work together, Jennifer has been able to identify the old "enemies" of her creative self-worth and the messages from the past that have affected her creative life. More important, she has now found all the positive messages from her current "fans" of her creativity and is moving toward incorporating the positive messages from these individuals as an important part of her creative identity and work.

During our last session, Jennifer's new-found confidence also helped her to make a decision about the podcast project. In her small community, she found that emerging writers were in need of help to move forward with their creativity. There were few resources in the area to help these writers learn the art of writing and crafting stories. Jennifer felt that these writers needed guidance, and as a result, she made the decision not to move forward with the podcast project but instead channel her energy and time to a workshop series for her community on expressive writing. In addition to rediscovering her creative identity, the process opened her to finding a new purpose for her talents.

Learning Points

1. To pursue a creative life, it is important to know your creative identity and know how it reflects in your endeavors. When we know our creative identity, we become clearer on the projects and activities that feel right for us.
2. Actively taking a role in finding your inner critic, discovering the origins, and taking steps to silence it can be important before wading into new projects that are new and challenging.
3. A reminder of who supports your creativity helps to undergird your creative efforts, especially in times of doubt.

Self-Coaching Questions

1. How do you feel about yourself as a creative individual?
2. If you do not feel that you are creative, what or who in your past challenged your thoughts on your creative identity? If you had the opportunity, what would you say to the people who discouraged your creativity?
3. Who currently and in your past encouraged or praised your creativity? If you had the opportunity, what would you say to these people in gratitude? Try writing out affirmations to challenge any negative thoughts about your creative identity. For example, if you believe that "I need to go to art school to be considered an artist," you might want to write, "I am an artist because of my talent, passion, and enthusiasm." How can you use your affirmations to guide and affirm you on a daily basis?

About Sharon J. Burton

Sharon J. Burton is an artist, art curator, and creative life advisor and founder of Spark Your Creative Coaching based in the Washington, DC, area. She is a mixed media visual artist whose preferred medium is collage and has exhibited her art in galleries, art venues, and other settings across the country since 2007. Sharon has curated a number of art exhibitions featuring emerging artists since 2005 and has served as an art consultant for novice art collectors.

Since 2016, she has focused on helping people in "creative recovery," those looking to revive or jumpstart their creativity through workshops, her blog, and as the host of the podcast Spark Your Creative (formerly The Mindfully Creative Podcast), which features artists and other creatives who are using their unique talents to create more mindful communities and a safer world. In 2017, Sharon launched Spark Your Creative Coaching (www.sparkyour creative.com) to provide services for individuals looking to discover or rediscover their creative gifts. You can view her art at www.sjbcreativeart.com.

Small, Simple, and Every Day

17

Constructing a Creative Life

Stephanie Christie

Tessa loved to write and couldn't help but create elaborate, insightful stories. She had already self-published two novels but wanted her third to get the recognition she felt had eluded her.

Tessa was clear on the steps she needed to take. She generally completed projects to an excellent standard. She was also emotionally self-aware, aided by regular journaling. There was only one problem.

Tessa doubted she was a 'real' writer.

According to Tessa, 'real' writers were disciplined, working long, strict hours every day. Tessa, in contrast, hadn't been doing much for her creativity lately. A mother with a full-time job, she showed a common creative pattern: obsession when working on a project, dropping off to nothing for months (or years) in between.

I asked Tessa if she missed writing. She replied, "Writing is really important to me. But I don't want to do it right now—it's not the right time." She had a range of valid reasons why.

Tessa wanted my support to help her brave putting her work into the public eye. And, more immediately, how on earth would she do the zillion things that needed to be done to self-publish, at the right time, in the right order, without blowing a mental fuse?

Tessa was struggling to take action. She couldn't face the first task she'd set herself, to edit the current draft of her manuscript, readying it for final proofing. And she was neglecting simple ways to move forward, focusing instead on the things that scared her (such as: "How will I manage a book launch, when even walking into a bookshop full of successful novels makes me feel sick?").

Stories of doom often featured in our early conversations. She told me, "I'm not an insider, so the establishment won't support me." One day she said, "Maybe I really am lazy, like I was told as a kid." What a rough thing to say to somebody—especially yourself!

I sensed these were protective mechanisms, Tessa's brain trying to keep her safe from the new risks she was contemplating. We talked about treating herself gently. Tessa was held back by real blocks, but the answer wasn't to push harder or be more disciplined. We needed to make the blocks smaller until they felt easy to overcome.

Tessa wanted accountability, so I suggested: "Every week, you let me know what you want to have done by our next session. If you do it, great. If you don't, that's useful information for us. We'll work together to break those things down into smaller parts. If you get stuck, I have techniques to try until we find what works."

Tessa had struggled with the question: how do I share this novel? We turned it into: how can the work of sharing this novel be made manageable and motivating?

It was time for Tessa to engage with the novel again after months away from it. She'd built up a resistance to this and even questioned whether editing was necessary. I suggested that if she wanted to do what was best for the novel, she'd be wise to at least look it over.

We talked about the stages involved in this process, making each as tiny as we could. Step one became: "Put the manuscript on my table where I can see it." Because people with high expectations of themselves can get overwhelmed and do nothing, I assured Tessa that taking any step was a triumph in this situation.

The next week, Tessa reported: "I'm really enjoying working through the chapters of this novel and realizing how good it is! I can't wait to get it published."

I was delighted by this breakthrough. "What got you started on the editing?"

"I was walking past the manuscript and thought I'd just have a peek inside. I started reading—then worked on it all weekend!"

As the self-publishing got underway, Tessa had more and more to do. She began to forget things she'd said she'd do between sessions.

I asked her, "Do you have a to-do list?"

"I've tried it," she told me, "but I just end up losing the piece of paper."

Choosing a simple system makes organization easier. I asked her, "If you had one place you kept track of all your tasks, what would make you want to use it?"

She said, "If I had a nice notebook and put it open on my desk, I'd see it every time I walked past. Actually, I got given a gorgeous notebook for my birthday . . . I'll use that."

"Perfect," I said. "It's easy to forget to look at the list though, so could you link that to any other activity you do every day? That way the list stays fresh in your mind."

Tessa paused and then replied, "Well, there's a quiet patch after dinner, before the kids go to bed. I can train myself to check it then. There might even be time to cross something off it."

With this structure in place, Tessa's ability to take action accelerated.

As Tessa's self-publishing adventure gained momentum, she achieved a long-held dream of seeing her novel in a big bookstore. She received rave reviews, hosted a well-attended book launch, and built a devoted social media following. "I'm the same person as I was before, though. Maybe there's no such thing as an insider," she finally told me.

After completing her original goal, Tessa said she wanted to keep up the momentum she'd gained during our time together. She had three novels in development, all at different stages. But how could she work without the deadline that had been driving her?

We analyzed what kind of activities each project required. We talked over the various times Tessa had available to work (including her likely energy levels). Then we matched the two up, making a plan she could stick to.

I noticed that all of Tessa's tasks involved working with existing materials— editing, arranging, polishing, filling gaps. Tessa often brought up her idea for a new novel but would always repeat that she'd work on it one day in the future. It was as if she craved going back into the world of creating a story but was scared of it as well.

Now seemed a good time to come back to my earlier question: do you miss sitting down and writing? To bring it up, I talked about my own daily writing practice: how it makes me so happy to go into that creative zone and how it helps the rest of my day shine.

Tessa said that sounded wonderful, so I asked her if she'd like to leave reality behind for a moment and imagine something. If there was a way that she could write a little every day, when would it be, and how would it work?

Tessa thought for a while before replying. "I'd leave a note for myself by my computer at night, about a scene or character I want to explore. Then I'd get up in the morning before the kids and write for half an hour."

"I love the idea of leaving yourself a writing prompt!" I said. "If you ever want to give this a go, I'd suggest setting your expectations low enough that even on a bad day, you can still meet them. That way you keep the habit going."

"So, like 15 minutes, and then I could extend it upwards if I want." Tessa spoke quickly.

"You seem curious. Do you think you'd like to try this, to see what happens?"

Tessa undertook this experiment the next day. And the next. She's been writing every morning since. Being in the creative zone brings her joy and meaning she'd forgotten she missed.

This, more than putting her book out there, more than great reviews, and more than fans, has let Tessa know in her heart that she is a real writer.

Learning Points

1. Structure is more effective than discipline. It's also easier to set up a structure than it is to rewire yourself to be more disciplined. Building a structure to support your creativity makes going into the creative zone possible even when stress is high or motivation seems nonexistent.

2. Often, what looks like a huge challenge is actually made up of a whole lot of easy steps, with a few unknown or scary steps thrown in. Break it down! You can always get help with the tricky parts.

3. You can bring creativity back into your life! Things change, and you may need to invent new ways to create based on your current life, but you can do this. If you miss creativity, today is the best possible day to get started.

Self-Coaching Questions

1. What structures can you put in place to make it easy for you to do your creative work? Daily routines, a diary, accountability, rituals, a to-do list, boundaries, and even alarms on your phone can help. This can't be discovered by theorizing. Keep experimenting until you find what works.

2. If you're stuck, how can you change your question to be more helpful? For example, "How do I do X?" can become: "How can I structure the work required to do X in a way that suits me?"

3. If you struggle to step into the creative identity you crave, are you consistently connecting with your creativity? If not, take all your reasons why not and seal them in an imaginary box for five minutes. Now tell me—if you could connect daily with your creativity, what would that look like?

About Stephanie Christie

Stephanie helps women who are frustrated with sidelining their creativity to get back into the creative zone and to make and share work they love. She believes creativity can be easy! After you build your structure, support systems, and self-belief, it needs only be as hard as the creative challenges you choose for yourself. Stephanie is a creative coach, poet, and artist. She works one on one over the phone (or Internet). You can find handy tips and get in touch with her at www.stephaniechristiecreative.com.

A Writer in Search of a Practice

18

How Coaching Launched a Hundred Consecutive Days of Writing

Jude Walsh

Amelie expressed interest in my Writing Mindset class but was unable to attend at the scheduled time. After chatting with her by phone, I offered to meet her for a private coaching session.

She was quite successful in her current working life as a television producer. She had just completed a project in which she wrote narrative for a program that received several prestigious awards. But . . . she longed to finish a short story and a novel that she began several years ago. She, in her words, "is just now connecting the dots and realizing that the narrative project at work derailed my personal writing practice." She was very hard on herself, sharing that it was not only that she didn't have enough time to write but also that she wrestled with the demons of "no one will want to read this anyway" and "it's not very good."

On the other hand, she also commented, "If I don't get published, that's okay because I've done something that makes me happy. So now the question is . . . why am I not doing something that I enjoy and that makes me happy?" She had put up so many obstacles that she was frozen.

I identified two elements to focus on in this session: finding enough time to write and establishing a steady practice. My plan was to ferret out her most immediate writing issue and then focus on it in a brief burst of focused writing, demonstrating how much she could accomplish in a short time.

We began by my asking her to tell me one thing she was struggling with in her novel. She identified a plot point that troubled her. I asked her to write down her question about that plot point and then to immediately begin writing possible answers. There was to be no hesitating, she was to keep her pen moving, and all thoughts were to go down no matter how bizarre they seemed. I allowed her 11 minutes to write. At the end of the time, she came up smiling. When we counted her words, almost 200, it was more than she had written the entire week before.

This was fun for her! For our next step, we explored a mantra she could use to help herself "drop" into the writing. The two reasons she had not been productive were that she was not carving time out to write and that she judged her writing in a negative way. We agreed that quality was not the goal; the goal was getting words on the page. For the mantra, we settled on "I don't feel like writing now, *and* I am going to write anyway."

Next was a deep dive into her work schedule and her family schedule, so as to find the time to write. Since we had established that she could get hundreds of words down in 11 minutes, this task turned out to be relatively easy. We looked for a way for her to block off 30 minutes a day for writing. She decided that she could stop on her way home from work at the very coffee shop where we were meeting and write. She knew her partner would not mind starting their family time a bit later.

Then I coached her to set a short-term goal. She decided to aim for 30 consecutive days of writing. I had two postcards with me that I had her address to herself. I asked her to fill out the first one right there, with a note congratulating herself on her accomplishment, and to mail it immediately. Yes, she would get it before her 30 days were up; that was the magic. I told her to post it near her computer as soon as it arrived. The second postcard I would send her at a later date for some surprise encouragement.

As a bonus, I gave her a small bottle of an essential oil blend that I had created with her in mind. I encouraged her to dab some on her wrists at the beginning of each writing session, the idea being to associate that particular smell with creativity and to provide a sensory-connected ritual to step into her writing time.

Amelie was brimming with optimism when she left this coaching session. She made those first 30 days with ease. Then 60. Then 90. We recently celebrated her 100th day of consecutive writing. Her book is well in hand. She has a writing practice that sustains her. She believes in herself as a writer again. Sometimes just one coaching session is enough to change a writer's life.

Learning Points

1. Allow yourself to take one small step at a time and know that it is enough. Remind yourself that simply by doing one thing, you are already vastly ahead of the many people who never take that one step. You are doing better than you think you are.
2. Congratulate yourself in advance for making progress. Do something that indicates to you that it has already occurred. For example, send yourself a post card congratulating yourself on having surpassed one of your goals. Send it BEFORE you hit the goal.
3. Have strategies in place to make the experience sensory, engaging one of the five senses. Select an essential oil blend that you smell, spray, or diffuse to set the stage for writing or a specific candle scent that you only burn while creating. Let that smell trigger your creative mojo.

Self-Coaching Questions

1. What are the obstacles keeping me from my definition of success? List every single thing you are telling yourself. Now rewrite each of those and add "and I am going to do it anyway, and *here is how.*" Do not be afraid of outside-of-the-box solutions; they often present the perfect answer.
2. When I have what I want, how will I feel? How will my life be different? Using the most sensory words you have, describe that. Can you sink into that feeling? Can you internalize it? Even if you can only feel it for a few seconds, you are well on your way to reprogramming your brain.
3. What is the one thing I can do today to move me toward my desire? Step away from making the long list of things to do to get to your goal. Focus on the *one* do-able thing in this moment. And when it is finished, pause and appreciate the fullness of that before moving on to the next thing. Do the first step, then the next step, to propel yourself forward.

About Jude Walsh

Jude Walsh is a creativity and life coach, writer, and writing teacher. She teaches classes on writing mindset and legacy writing (personal essays for seniors wishing to pass down stories). As a coach, she especially likes working with women post divorce or men and women wishing to reinvent themselves creatively and pivot to a new life. Her superpower is that she can see the best in a person and then help them see it and believe it too. She has numerous essays published in literary magazines and anthologies. She is the author of *Post-Divorce Bliss: Ending Us and Finding Me* (Morgan James Press, 2019).

We're All in This Together

19

How Group Creativity Coaching Provides Support

Doreen Marcial Poreba

It's hard to live the dream when you're not even sure what the dream is. Ideas form with no follow-through, thoughts lacking focus rush in and out, and once-passionate desires lose their direction.

Not exactly the stuff that dreams are made of, but then again, these misfires are often the starting point for those who are being honest with themselves as they participate in my creativity group sessions.

Upon hearing about my group sessions, Jonah felt they might be helpful. "I was feeling like a frustrated artist in that I was limited to doodling and dabbling," he said. "The creativity sessions sounded intriguing, and I thought to myself, 'Let's see what this is.'"

Jonah was one of 10 people who signed up for one of my 13-week creativity group coaching processes. I always begin my group sessions by having the participants introduce themselves and state their intention. What do they wish to create as a result of going through these sessions?

Jonah described himself as a person who liked to "stretch a bit," and his specific intention was to develop more as an artist and, more generally, to expand his creativity. Admittedly, he had no idea what he was getting into, but he'd always had an affinity for group processes and taking on new challenges.

"I was cautiously optimistic, and I had no way of anticipating how my inner artist, my creative self, would be unleashed," said Jonah. "I had a frame of reference, a self-view, whereas I had an idea about who I was creatively, but I found that my creative inclinations still never much blossomed."

About three weeks into the group process, Jonah made a connection to a negative past experience. He recalled that his brother could paint, sculpt, and draw and was the one perceived by his family as the artist. This revelation, this memory from his past, provided much needed clarity for him.

"That whole misconception of myself, which was a construct of mine, got cemented into place pretty early," he said. "In reality, I wasn't necessarily limited or confined. . . . I was in my self-created box."

I always make it a point to stress the confidentiality of all that is shared in my groups, and Jonah expressed how this allowed him to explore in a safe space.

"Being in a group, there's this exploration that you're not the only one who has self-limiting beliefs. I had buried that memory. It was very subconscious . . . my brother's the artist, not me, and I had never verbalized that out loud before. The discussions helped get it unburied, and I saw how it helped open everyone else up, too."

He also spoke about how sharing this memory helped to illuminate new areas for consideration so that he could break out.

"Illumination of what's possible made the opening," he said. "All I needed was an opening. There wasn't anything in my past to open a new window."

One of the most useful tools that Jonah cited was what author Julian Cameron calls 'morning pages' in her classic creativity book *The Artist's Way*. It's a tool that I introduce to my groups as a basic tenet of the creativity process that everyone in the group commits to doing until at least the end of the 13 weeks.

'Morning pages' entails writing three pages every morning of longhand, stream of consciousness writing. The idea is to get out all of the thoughts and feelings that might be getting in the way of your creativity.

Although Jonah said he benefited greatly from committing himself to writing morning pages every day, that process wouldn't have been nearly as effective if he hadn't considered the fact that he had limited himself because of his own self-image. What needed work was opening his mind and his heart.

The group coaching process also helped him in a way that one might not have expected.

"What I love about group processes is that I'm a little competitive," he said. "In a group process, I get a real kick out of the thought, 'Let's see what I can do.' Having 'bragging rights' in a group adds fuel to my fire as opposed to being alone in my garage."

I remember that Jonah was the first one in the group to enter the fourth session with a creative work that he wished to share. At that point, I had not asked any of the participants to 'show and tell' because that usually happens later in the process. But Jonah was so excited that he decided to bring in his first painting sooner rather than later.

He exclaimed, "I did something! I have created something, and I'm so thrilled with it!"

As much as Jonah enjoyed writing every morning, he realized that painting provided the most fun. He described to the other participants that he discovered how much he liked experimenting with colors.

"I like writing and sculpting, but painting is more fun than anything for me. I like color and didn't realize how fun it is to play with color."

Another basic tenet that I introduce to my groups also comes from Julia Cameron's *The Artist's Way*—the idea of the 'artist date,' which is intended to ignite the imagination.

I directed Jonah and the others to go on a once-a-week journey by themselves doing something that interested them, perhaps an activity they'd never done before. As Cameron puts it, the 'artist date' does not need to be artistic. Rather, she states, "Think mischief more than mastery."

Each week, the participants would report on their 'artist date,' and Jonah shared that his most memorable one was dressing up in his finest suit and going to a local restaurant by himself.

"I savored every minute of the whole thing," he said. "I never even conceived of doing that. It helped my creativity by honoring myself in ways that I hadn't done previously . . . by giving myself gifts, which meant I valued my worthiness. I could devote time and energy from my own inspiration, just for that."

Throughout the 13-week coaching process, I ended each session with a hands-on activity that allowed the participants to explore their creativity while also getting the benefit of bonding with others in the group.

"Giving myself the gift of inspiration on a regular basis is just incredibly powerful," said Jonah. "These group coaching sessions helped me get in a groove and stay inspired."

Jonah went on to bring a number of paintings to share with the group and was so inspired by the group creativity sessions that he enrolled two more times over a three-year period.

Because of the confidence and support he gained from participating in the creativity sessions, he ended up walking away from a 20-year career to one that allowed him to use his creative skills as both a painter and a home designer, and he's in the process of writing three books. He attributes his expansion to his time spent with the groups.

"I learned there's a place for creativity everywhere—the studio, the boardroom, and the bedroom, and I'm more unstoppable than I've ever been, thanks to the creativity coaching," said Jonah.

Learning Points

1. Don't go it alone. If you're hesitant about doing one-on-one coaching, consider a group process in which you'll have additional support and encouragement.
2. There are many tools of the trade. Whether you're feeling stuck creatively or simply wish to expand your creativity, there are many tools you'll learn during a group process, both from the creativity coach and others in the group because of the synergy that gets created from the interactions among multiple participants.
3. Venture out of your norm. During the group process, be open to going beyond your past experiences. During the first session of one of my groups, I had a participant completely resist the idea of the 'artist date.' I encouraged her to drop her guard and to simply give it a chance. She came to the next session and couldn't wait to tell the group about not one artist date but two!

Self-Coaching Questions

1. Consider whether you feel more comfortable discussing your creativity challenges one on one with a creativity coach or whether you feel you would benefit more from a group process facilitated by a coach. It's also possible to do both. Know thyself and what you feel would work best for you.
2. Give yourself permission to find your voice. As a creativity coach, if I see participants sitting silently, I specifically invite them into the conversation. The old adage applies, "The more you put into your creativity coaching experience, the more you'll get out of it."
3. Let your faith in the creativity coaching process replace your fears. I have been amazed by the progress my group participants have made, both personally and professionally, after going through the creative group process. You can, too! Also, it's important to understand that creativity is not limited to the arts. Although artistic talents such as painting, singing, dancing, and playing an instrument are great examples of creativity, there are many other areas where creativity comes into play. Ask yourself, "What do I wish to create in my life, and what is keeping me from achieving that?"

Doreen Marcial Poreba

Doreen Marcial Poreba's entire career has revolved around creativity, first as a TV news reporter and then as an award-winning, accredited, public relations professional and photographer. In 2014, she completed an intensive program by the Creativity Coaching Association to become a Certified Creativity Coach and now provides individual and group creativity sessions. She is the author of two books, and she draws much of her creative inspiration from her time spent as a singer-songwriter and musician. Visit Doreen's website at www.creativecaboose.com or connect with her via Facebook at www.facebook.com/certifiedcreativitycoach.

A Whirlwind Trapped in a Coffee Cup

20

Fearing Art-Making When Art Is Linked to Suffering

Beatriz Martínez Barrio

I met Alicia at a portfolio review. She had recently graduated from art college and was starting her career as an artist. She was photographing performative actions that exerted a subtle violence on the body as it was pushed to its limits. The work was intense and emotional, revealing struggle and pain.

The next time I saw her was at my office six years later. The first thing she said was:

> I haven't produced any work since that portfolio review. I simply stopped. I had such a crazy emotional life at that time. I felt like a small boat in the middle of the ocean being carried away by the waves. Everything was so intense: the love, the pain, the guilt. . . . I just broke down. I realized that I needed help and started therapy. I feel I'm a healthier person now, but I've lost my motivation to create.

I suggested an exercise to Alicia. I showed her a set of photographs and asked her to choose one that represented her creative energy. She chose a photomontage of a coffee cup with a whirlwind inside. I asked her to describe the image.

"It's a whirlwind, wild and crazy, trapped in a coffee cup. It doesn't belong here. It should be in the ocean, but it doesn't know how to get there."

I asked her to say the same sentence in first person.

"I'm a whirlwind, wild and crazy, trapped in a coffee cup." Her eyes filled with tears.

"Do you feel your creative energy that way?"

"I do. I feel it is wild and crazy, and it scares me. I fear that if I start to create again, I'm going to go back to that crazy emotional life. But if I don't, I will feel a part of me is dead. When I finished school, I really believed that I could be an artist and had things to say, but now I feel I don't have anything interesting to talk about."

"How do you know if something is interesting enough to be talked about?"

"I guess when it is dramatic. I've always thought drama was my source of inspiration. My best work was produced when I was hurting the most."

"No wonder you don't want to create! It seems you have a belief that good creations are based on pain. That is not an unusual belief. We have a cultural history that links art and suffering."

We talked about the prejudices of what an artist should be, and we worked on reframing the negative beliefs. Alicia used art as a channel of expression for her inner world that was filled with pain. Now she could choose to express other feelings, sensations, or thoughts, but she didn't know which. Drama had given her the motivation to create, and now she no longer felt the urge. For our next session, I suggested that she make a selection of artwork that she admired so we could analyze what these works had in common and look for new themes and sources of inspiration.

When I saw the selection, the first thing that caught my attention was that in most of the images, there was a duality or a contrast between two things. When I pointed this out to her she was surprised. She hadn't chosen them for those reasons, but she agreed that there was a pattern in her choices. I asked her how she felt about that.

"I guess I've always felt divided inside: my head says one thing, and my gut says the opposite. Therapy has helped me find a dialogue between them, but it is still not easy for me."

"How does this relate to your creativity?"

"I guess I feel the same division inside. If I'm an artist, I feel crazy and out of control, and if I'm healthy, I can't create."

She also mentioned that she had mixed feelings about the work that she had produced while she was in college. Some of her performances were violent actions against herself, and she feared this self-destructive side. She hadn't forgiven herself for things she had done in the past and still felt a lot of guilt and shame.

"I think you are being self-destructive by denying your creative energy," I told her.

Her face became serious, and she kept silent.

"How do you feel about what I've just told you?"

"It hurts. I've never thought I was being self-destructive by denying my creative energy."

"It seems you have a conflict with a part of yourself, and you have linked that part to your creative energy. But maybe there are other ways to see this polarity. How would you name these two parts of yourself?"

"The dark side and the healthy side."

I recommended she explore this duality through a written dialogue between her right hand and her left hand. She could start by asking a question to the dark side with her dominant hand and let her nondominant side write down the answer. She felt awkard in the beginning but eventually became very involved with the exercise. She realized that the dark side was quite angry because it had been repressed and judged for so long. She was also surprised to find out that her healthy side was rigid, controlling, and a perfectionist. The dark side was spontaneous, creative, and had a sense of humor. She smiled saying:

"I guess the dark side isn't that bad after all."

"It's like the yin/yang symbol. There's always some light in the shadow and some shadow in the light. Ideally, you could have both sides working together toward your goal. How do you think you could achieve this? What does your dark side need from your healthy side to start creating? Can you ask her?"

She began writing again, and after a few minutes, she said: "The healthy side is scared that we are going to be hurt again, but the dark side has answered that we are not the same person that we were six years ago and are not trusting our own growth."

I smiled and said with excitement, "What a wise answer! I do agree with your dark side! What steps do you think you can take next week to reconnect with your creativity? Maybe something small and not too scary?"

She thought for a while and then answered, "Maybe I could take the camera out and shoot some pictures!" She smiled.

"It seems this thought makes you happy! Any ideas of where you would go or what you would want to photograph?"

"Maybe some lights and shadows?" We both laughed.

For a month, Alicia worked on a series of self-portraits with lights and shadows projected on her body. She was able to reconcile with her inner artist, which was not only filled with pain, suffering, and craziness but also with passion, vitality, and freedom. As the process developed, other types of fear started to appear, such as the fear of being narcissistic for doing self-portraiture and the fear of not being good enough. She was very insecure and had a strongly critical inner voice. We worked on these issues until one day she arrived very agitated and shared: "Something happened and I'm embarrassed to tell you." She bit her lip. "I've been unfaithful. I went to a concert, drank too much, and ended up in bed with this guy. I don't know why I did it. I don't even like him that much. I love my boyfriend. I feel terrible. It's my dark side taking control again! I knew it would eventually happen."

I was concerned when I heard Alicia's confession. I feared that this event would be the proof she needed to confirm that creativity was emotionally dangerous for her. To me, it seemed clear that the action had been a self-sabotage, a kind of test she needed to overcome. But I was not sure whether she could do it. She blamed her inner artist for her behavior, and in doing so, she avoided taking responsibility for her actions. She found reasons to keep the pattern of being a destructive, blocked artist.

At our next session, she told me that she and her boyfriend had had a big argument. They had almost broken off their relationship but somehow found a way to stay together. She was still scared, but she realized she had dealt with the situation very differently than six years ago. It seemed therapy had done its work. She was still repeating some of her old patterns, but she was also reacting and behaving differently. We focused on how she could continue being creative while at times still feeling like she was in the middle of the tsunami. Some days she felt better and other days worse, but she was able to build some work routine and continued shooting pictures.

One day she told me that she had a dream. She saw herself in a thunderstorm in the middle of the ocean. She was being tossed by the waves with no control, and she knew it was only a matter of time before she would drown. "The funny thing was that the boat I was riding was a coffee cup!" she laughed. "Then something magical happened, I realized there was a spoon by my side, so I put it into the water and turned it into a tiller. . . . I was then able to surf the waves!"

I smiled and thought that her subconscious had given her such a beautiful image of her personal and creative process.

Learning Points

1. Beneath a creative blockage usually lies a fear.
2. Creative processes as well as personal processes grow in a spiral. It seems we are going in circles, but we are moving forward toward another turn of the spiral.

3. Two techniques:
   a. Use of photographs as projective tools to increase self-knowledge and awareness
   b. Use of written dialogue between left and right hand to explore and integrate polarities and connect to inner voice and wisdom

---

Self-Coaching Questions

1. What are your beliefs and prejudices about what an artist should be?
2. What is your "shadow part" as an artist? What do you fear the most?
3. What is your "creative tiller"? What resources do you have that can help you create in the middle of life's waves?

Beatriz Martínez Barrio

Beatriz Martínez Barrio is a visual artist and art therapist based in Madrid, Spain. She uses art as an introspective and healing tool to help people reconnect with their own source of creativity and wisdom. She specializes in creative processes that involve the use of photography and video. For more than a decade, she has been coordinating the Master of Photography course at EFTI School of Photography in Madrid, where she helps students find their strengths in the visual languages. She also uses photography and art in her private art therapy sessions and creativity workshops. She collaborates as a professor in various art therapy schools in Madrid. For more information, visit www.beatrizmbarrio.com.

A Colorless World   **21**

How Creativity Coaching Restored Vibrancy to One Painter's Life

Natalie Dadamio

When Adam came to me, he was feeling defeated, worn down, and hopeless. He hadn't created anything in several years and was finding it hard to come to terms with starting over.

"It's been so long since I created anything, and the last time I painted, I was still in a really dark place. I just don't know if I can create anything again."

I told him that I understood where he was coming from, and I asked him to think back to the last time he was creating and, from that recollection, to describe to me what that had felt like.

Adam explained to me that although he was in a whirlwind of pain and confusion and heavy into a party lifestyle, he loved painting, and it was the only time that he felt free.

After making the decision to clean up his lifestyle, he felt that he lost touch with his creativity and in turn lost the feeling of freedom that it provided.

During the years that Adam wasn't creating, however, he spent time focusing on his mental, emotional, and spiritual health. He sought help for his personal issues, and it helped heal a lot of pain from past trauma and experiences.

Adam came to me because he had known personally that I took a lot of the same steps in my own life. It was important to him that he work with someone who understood the struggle to restore not only health and vitality back to one's life but also one's own inherit creativity.

I wanted to make sure Adam knew that he was strong for making the healthy choices that he did, and I reassured him that all parts of our lives take time and patience to cultivate.

I discussed with him the idea of journaling and expressed how helpful it had been in my own journey, and I asked him if he would be willing to start a journal with the intention of reigniting his creativity.

The task was simple enough, to record the wonders of his daily life. Some examples that I gave him where the following: the way a bird soars in the sky; the way the wind whistles hello; or perhaps a favorite book, poem, or song. In truth, it could be anything that stood out to him, from the mundane to the extraordinary.

At first, Adam was a bit apprehensive. He was wondering why he should start a journal when his goal was to paint. I explained to him that when things have been deadened or blocked off for a long period of time, it can be hard to recapture the memories and moments that once filled us with joy and liveliness.

This journaling exercise is something that encourages one to reopen to things they love in order to start to feed the spirit again and ultimately help reengage creativity. By recording the wonders and looking at the world in this way, it can help to open the gateway to the genuine expression that has naturally been present all along.

Adam agreed to start the journal and to meet again in two weeks to discuss what he recorded.

"So, how did it go?" I asked when we met.

"Okay, I guess," Adam replied sheepishly.

"Well, would you like to tell me any wonders you recorded?"

"Yeah, sure" Adam replied, as he flipped through his journal. "One wonder is that I love to sing. I sing and sing even if it doesn't make sense."

"That's great, Adam. Is there any particular time that you sing, or are you in a specific location?"

"Well, I like to be alone when I am singing, so in the car, or out in nature, or even in the shower, and of course, when no one is home. I feel more comfortable when I am alone."

"That's wonderful. Is there anything else in your journal you would like to share?"

"Another wonder is that I love trees. I love the shapes of the way they are constructed, how they grow towards the light, how they are gnarly, and all over the place. I love how they are all interconnected and have deep roots, and how they are connected to the earth yet reach to the stars."

Adam looked at me with a twinkle in his eye as if this one wonder conjured up so many things.

"That's really fantastic, Adam! I love the imagery you created with the trees. When you were looking at and considering the trees, did you feel anything specifically? Did any emotions arise or a general sense within yourself?"

"Well, I was thinking about the interconnection of all things, they remind me of the synapses in the brain, like a web of creation. A memory came up for me when I was a small child around the age of five or six, I remember loving to stare up at the trees and watch the leaves blow and how it used to make me laugh. I imagined what it would be like to be a leaf blowing in the wind. The trees made me feel safe."

"That's great! Is there anything else? You seem to be on a roll here."

"Yes, there is a little more here." Adam said as he thumbed through the marked pages. "I love the way the mist rolls off the river in an early morning light. It's grey, cloudy, and milky, like fluffy storm clouds. It's haunting yet inviting. And I love the wonder of the night sky and the wonder of the tiniest insect, and I love the way the cracks in the cement happen to create patterns. And the way the sunlight on water creates ripples of dots."

"How do they make you feel?" I asked.

"Well, uh, uh . . . I don't really know," Adam stammered.

"Well, I'd like to try something that might help. I would like to bring you into a more relaxed state, so that you can access your deepest wisdom, if that's okay?"

"Sure," Adam agreed.

"I'd like you to close your eyes and take a few deep breaths."

I did the exercise along with him, to help hold and open the space by creating the connection.

"Now, with your eyes closed, can you tell me how recording the wonders made you feel? Just say the first thing that comes to mind and don't worry what it is. There are no wrong answers; we're just looking for your initial response."

"Well, I feel light, floaty, sort of dreamy like," he responded.

"That's great, Adam. What else?"

"I feel like the light dancing on the river is rippling through my body, and the mist rolling off the river is like a release from the past. I can see the swirling images of abstract shapes, color, and form. I can feel that the images that I am drawn to have a story to tell. They feel comforting."

"That sounds excellent, Adam. Is there anything else that the wonders make you feel?"

Adam took a deep breath, let out a sigh, and said, "The wonders make me feel connected again. I feel connected to myself and to that freedom."

All along I had been breathing and feeling his replies as Adam expressed his natural wonders, the things that made him come alive, and I could hear and feel the transformation in him as we talked.

"Okay, Adam, now when I count to three, I want you to slowly open your eyes. One, coming back to the room. Two, slowly feeling your body. Three, opening your eyes. Now, how do you feel? Are you ready for your next step?"

Adam was a bit groggy yet alert enough to eagerly ask for the next step.

"Okay, great. The next step is to take the feeling of the wonders you accessed today, go home, and paint something from that state."

"But I don't know if I am ready to paint," Adam said hesitantly.

I assured Adam that he was ready and that there was no expected outcome. It was simply another steppingstone in the path of reigniting his creativity. If he felt doubtful, he could remember today's session and access the feelings that arose in the meditation, or he could revisit the pages of his journal of wonders and rekindle that connection.

I also let Adam know that he could reach me by email with any questions or concerns that might arise, that I would be available for him, so that he knew he wasn't on his own.

Adam agreed to try to paint. We set up another appointment to meet in two weeks.

The next time we met, Adam was filled with enthusiasm and excitement. The exercises had worked, and he had begun to paint again.

Now that he had reunited with his love for painting and restored color and vibrancy back to his life, he was ready to start making the long journey back and begin his life over again as an artist.

Learning Points

1. Sometimes a person must address and perhaps even clean up an area of his or her life before he or she can access another.
2. It takes courage to ask for help and to face one's blocks.
3. Creativity is as simple as tuning in, remembering, and accessing our own built-in guidance system.

Self-Coaching Questions

1. What is one area of your life that you might need to clean up and free up before you can move forward?

2. What small step could you take today that moves you closer to restoring the color within, or, in other words, the creative spirit within?

3. Close your eyes. Place your hand on your heart and take three deep breaths. Pull out your journal or a piece of paper. "What are your personal wonders?"

About Natalie Dadamio

Natalie Dadamio returned to her art practice after a long period of doubt, frustration, and misdirection. She knows what it is like to be stuck, fearful, and unsure about her own creativity and art making. It is this personal experience that fuels her interest and passion in helping others return to their inherent creativity.

Natalie has extensive training in the Shamanic healing arts and sees creativity as a soulful act. She desires to bring the two together in a unique and diverse way, while shedding new light on what it means to not just create art but also to live artfully. Information about her creativity coaching can be found online at www.creationsdreaming.com. Her artwork can be found online at www.nataliedadamio.com.

Art as Money　　　　　　**22**

Creating for Yourself and Not Just for Success

Steph Cohen

When James approached me for coaching, he was not confident it would be of any real help. He had a compulsion to change something in his life, but he was wary. He knew he wasn't happy and had traced the root cause of that unhappiness back to his lack of creative work, but he didn't feel confident that he could create again in a meaningful or transformative way.

We agreed to have a video call every two weeks with email communication in between. On our first call, he seemed resigned and cynical when discussing his creative fields of writing and sketching, and there was a lethargy in his approach to his own self-image as an artist. He'd had a successful career in journalism, but as time went on, he received fewer and fewer commissions until they dried up completely. He hadn't written any articles over the past couple of years and didn't miss it.

He had no desire to revisit the genre or fight his way to the top again. He had occasionally worked on small creative projects over the years but had no consistent practice and deep down felt like it was a waste of time if it wasn't earning him money. He had a family he needed to support and felt guilty if he spent his time on anything that wouldn't directly contribute to their well-being.

During our initial call, I asked him if he could tell me more about his idea that creativity wasn't worthwhile unless it had a positive financial outcome. He told me that both his parents came from modest backgrounds and had worked hard to provide. They took great pride in their son's academic achievements but displayed a certain level of dismissiveness for creative endeavors they considered to be frivolous. They encouraged him to focus on making a good living and committing his time and energy to things that would help him climb the ladder in life. Although he valued art and creativity, he'd always struggled to maintain a practice if he couldn't see tangible results.

I asked him what his goals were for the sessions, what his minimum outcome and big vision outcome might look like. His minimum goal was to create consistently, although he wasn't sure what. His big vision goal was creating work of value that could replace or add to his income. We started by addressing his minimum goal. We discussed where he would create: at a small table in the corner of his home office on which he could draw or write. We discussed what time of day might be best for him: the end of his workday before his children arrived back from school. He decided to create for one hour on weekdays and on weekends when his children were at various classes and activities.

On our second call, James was excited. He had written every afternoon for the previous two weeks and felt invigorated to be doing rather than thinking about doing. He had decided to write a piece of fiction and was very much enjoying using his imagination and challenging himself to craft interesting characters and lively pieces of prose. He had been unable to work over the weekend and decided he'd been too ambitious setting himself a seven-day week and was content to keep it at five. He was happy with the volume of work he had accomplished in the previous weeks and had enjoyed letting his ideas percolate and develop over the weekends.

He also mentioned he'd been thinking about his relationship with his parents and money since our last chat and hadn't realized how strongly he was still holding on to the idea that work was only worthy if it culminated in financial gain or social success. He was concerned that he might be inadvertently passing this belief on to his own children, but he was still struggling to see real value in his creative endeavors.

Despite enjoying his writing time, he still experienced underlying guilt that he wasn't dedicating that time to paying clients and still didn't really believe that his writing was worth anything or worthy in and of itself. I asked him if he would be willing to write an alternative goals list, a list of all the things he could achieve with his creativity outside of financial or social success. He agreed that he could definitely give this a go, though he initially felt that he didn't have anything to put on the list.

When I emailed to check in with James between our second and third call, he replied to say he was not doing so well. He hadn't written or drawn anything all week. In fact, he hadn't stuck to his afternoon schedule at all and had allowed work to spill over into his creative time because he felt compelled to choose practical work over frivolous creative time. He had decided that he couldn't write an alternative goals list because he couldn't persuade himself there really were any worthwhile goals beyond financial success.

He'd felt great resistance to continuing with his story because his old demon of 'What's the point?' had reared its ugly head. If his story could not earn him money or a great reputation as a writer, what was the point of dedicating time to it? He was back in his usual spiral of not creating and deeming any creative time unworthy.

I replied that perhaps figuring out the alternative payoffs he could get from creating might help him out of his current spiral because it would give him some very tangible reasons for doing what he loved outside of the financial. If this absolutely didn't work for him, then perhaps he might be able to think about creating a project with a view to selling it. But to achieve that financial goal, he needed the product, whether it was a short story, a novel, or a series of sketches—which meant dedicating time to creating.

I encouraged him to work through his resistance where the alternative goals list was concerned because it might prove useful in connecting him more deeply to his creative side, which could potentially enrich his work. He promised to try working on the list. He'd also realized that his afternoon time slot wasn't serving him well and announced that he would experiment with working early in the morning instead. He would move his desk closer to the window, where the natural light lifted his spirits, and he wouldn't allow his work papers to spill onto his dedicated creative space.

By the time we spoke again, he had made great strides. He had challenged himself to sit and work on his alternative goals list and had surprised himself with the outcome. He realized that one of the main things he wanted to instill in his children was the value of art on a personal level, the importance of creativity and imagination and the qualities of dedication, patience, and working with the ups and downs of making and experimenting. By encouraging their creative pursuits, letting them see him work on his art, sharing his artistic side with them, and spending time as a family making art, he could encourage them to embody many of the qualities he felt were important for them in life.

He also acknowledged that his own happiness was very much connected to his creative pursuits. Having a consistent outlet lifted his spirits, helped him to feel content in himself, patient, and open. He also knew that if he decided to make work to sell, it would take time and experimentation and that he had to commit himself to the chosen project to make it happen.

As James read his list aloud, he sounded much more connected to himself, grounded, and relaxed. I congratulated him on his work and suggested it might be a good idea to print out the list and keep it somewhere visible so he could refer to it whenever he needed.

During our final call, James told me that his new early morning routine was working well because his mind was clear of work concerns first thing in the morning, and he was excited to start the day using his imagination before settling into the regular rhythms of his client work. He hadn't yet found time to draw as much as he wanted, but he had made plans that weekend to have some family time when they would take a packed lunch and some art supplies to a nearby park. He was happy he was creating momentum with one of his creative passions and was content to figure out how to incorporate a second later down the line after solidifying his current practice.

Learning Points

1.   Underlying beliefs about the value of our work and creative impulses can often stop us from creating altogether.
2.   Ups and downs are a normal part of the creative process. There are points when our creative passions shift, we may not make any work for a while, and there may be a natural or challenging segue-way into another area of our creative life.
3.   Our workspace and surroundings can have a big effect on our ability to happily commit to creating. Sometimes a small change such as clearing clutter or letting in more light can make all the difference.

Self-Coaching Questions

1.   Can you identify people or circumstances in your life, past or present, that may be inadvertently stopping you from doing the work you really want?
2.   Can you identify times in your creative life when you have come to a natural end with a creative pursuit or passion? How did you respond to this? Did you go on to create in other ways?
3.   Do you feel excited or content in your workspace? Is there anything you can identify that you could change to help you create? Or, do you need to experiment with some new spaces entirely?

About Steph Cohen

Steph Cohen is an actress, writer, and creativity coach from the United Kingdom and based in Spain. She has a degree in English literature from Cambridge University, a degree in contemporary dance from Birkbeck and The Place, and has worked across multiple industries, including dance, literary publishing, finance, marketing, graphic design, and more. As well as pursuing her own creative career, Steph coaches artists of all disciplines to help them discover what works for them to create consistently and joyfully while achieving their deepest creative dreams. You can find out more at www.creative beingcoaching.com or email her at steph@creativebeingcoaching.com.

Helping a Designer Grow Her Confidence

23

Steps to a Design Career

Sally Mazák

Sarah was in her mid-20s. She had helped run a family antique business through her teens, had studied graphic design, and was a skilled realist painter. But when Sarah came to me, she had an overwhelming lack of confidence and "was too disorganized to sort out her life and her future."

During our first meeting, Sarah's worries spilled out, worries that were keeping her stuck in a nerve-wracking mental loop:

> I want to develop myself as a designer. I need to sort out what direction my life will take. I'm not sure that design is for me . . . maybe I want to take over my father's shop one day? I'm not sure. . . . I'm so envious when I see great creations in interiors, art and design, as I know I can do that too. . . . I just can't put it into practice. I need to learn some more skills. Maybe I should move back home. I'm so disorganized that I can't keep track. I need direction. . . . I get overwhelmed when I have too much design work going on in my freelance job at home and I have no boss to complain or vent to, only my husband, and this can be stressful on my relationship. . . . I work late at night because I waste all day getting lost in the Internet, then I have to work through the night to meet my deadlines . . . oh, and I keep forgetting to invoice!

There was a distinct lack of confidence in her voice. First, I assured her I was a safe person to vent to, with an understanding ear. As I listened, I noted her circling back repeatedly to her interest in the shop, her passion for design excellence, and her need to manage herself better.

Especially interesting to me was her admission of envy. When positively reframed, jealousy is often a remarkable road map to our deepest desires, so I made a note to circle back at some point to her comment, "I'm so envious when I see great creations in interiors, art and design, as I know I can do that too." Understanding exactly what Sarah thought she might be capable of accomplishing would be a helpful guide to knowing the best approach to coaching her out of her funk.

To get a better picture of her current situation and mostly to help her focus, I had Sarah fill in a short creativity coaching preparation form. Helping her form an overview of her feelings was a good measure of the present and something we could use to measure success in the future. Sometimes I use this form to lay the foundations for a more organized approach to coaching.

Sarah's current state was "tired; stuck; unsure; disorganized; afraid of taking action; running in circles; no time; feeling disconnected from purpose," and then a flip!

"Energized by a vision; excited about life; excited about the future; ready to try something new as what I'm doing isn't working; amazed at the things happening in my life."

What a surprise!

"Well we can work with that!" I said.

To clear her mind to make room for deeper work, Sarah was immediately introduced to the concept of free-flow writing—a tool to 'clear the bottleneck' of her thoughts and emotions. Privately writing with the wildest abandon she could muster, Sarah safely gave a voice to all her concerns. Then we began to chip away at the main issues gnawing at her confidence.

As a freelancer, most of Sarah's troubles lay in her difficulty in keeping track of her work hours and her own work value. She was a very talented designer, but she still felt like a 'junior' having to work to prove herself. Time would fly by, well into the night, and she would still be paid a flat rate of $300 for hours upon hours of detailed work. She felt as if she was the one responsible for 'being taken for a ride' by lacking the confidence to value and structure her time.

She also wasn't as upset, as one might imagine, by a low fee for complex work. Instead, she berated herself for her own unchecked loss of personal time and time with her fiancé. On top of this, she felt powerless to avoid the distractions of the Internet (an issue I hear from nearly every client), which meant she left the paid work until the last minute. Berating herself daily was an exhausting drain of her energy. We worked to resolve this situation as a priority.

The first goal to conquer was tracking her hours and efficiency, as any designer would in a studio scenario. Working for oneself can offer a more fluid lifestyle, which in this case was going too far, generating negative consequences.

We workshopped what she should be getting paid per hour in the industry, how many hours she would work to finish within the fee (she was comfortable with it covering about four or five hours), how she could get her speed up, and how her ideal schedule might look.

For her ideal schedule (*if anything were possible*), I taught her how to honor herself and simply test for a gut reaction: whether it felt good or not good. If she wasn't sure, then it certainly wasn't in the good category. You could usually tell if she was 'settling' because the response was a lackluster 'seems good.' I challenged her to adjust it to make it feel 'great'!

These little decisions gave her some much needed mental autonomy. Each time she would *cheekily* alter a plan to make it feel 'great,' she gained some maturity in her thinking and some control over her situation.

She explained: "I discovered that certain work methods and routines I employ aren't conducive to good practice for me. This can lead to frustration and creative blocking. I am still trying to master what works best for me, but I'm closer now than I ever was."

It took a number of months for her to experiment with her plan, work it, readjust it, and "master what works best for me"—but eventually, she got there. A major breakthrough was simply working in the day and not the night. "Mastering my working week" is what she called it. With support, these little adjustments created a healthy byproduct—more confidence.

Another contributing factor was her self-admitted overpoliteness. To stick up for herself felt 'aggressive' because this is what she had been taught. This was a crucial issue to resolve before she could progress effectively because it was blocking her ability to speak up for herself and take back some control—a factor that would play into her desire to be more organized. How can you be more organized if you can't articulate what you need, to others *and* to yourself?

One way to start practicing assertiveness and self-truth was to work on one of her objectives—"Not always agreeing to everyone else's terms"—so we set some teeny-tiny challenges to practice speaking up, starting in daily life.

Her main worry was being assertive without being aggressive. She knew she was in a safe space with me, so she could be completely open about how she felt about everything. We took it to another level. I regularly asked her basic probing questions such as "What do you *really* wish had happened in [that situation]?" and simply "What do you want?" She even surprised herself with her answers!

One week, her challenge was to speak her truth while shopping. This followed a conversation about her getting short changed and not mentioning it to the shop attendant. She was very polite, sweet, and humble . . . and it was making her suffer. That week she had to return something to a hardware store, and with polite self-assertion, she managed it! It was a major accomplishment, which, even though it sounds so simple, was a *huge* moment for her. And it created more of that healthy byproduct—confidence!

Guided coaching allowed Sarah the time to build on each session in a steady, safe, and practical way. Each small challenge allowed her time to adapt and grow. With a reduction in second guessing herself and the confidence to speak her truth, Sarah was able to make some clear, bold choices about her career.

Although seemingly uncertain of herself, on the contrary, Sarah had a high-level knowledge of the work she did. Only two years later, with her developed confidence, independent thinking, and practical skills, she merged her interests to form an exciting and thriving national business in contemporary design, which is now regularly featured in social media and magazines. This career decision was a natural amalgamation of her strengths, interests, and personal experiences, fueled by her clarity and a deep inner confidence.

Learning Points

1. Confidence is a byproduct of smaller actions. It is not always something you learn 'how to do' or 'get'; it can be gained by an accumulation process and 'baby steps.'
2. By having a regular commitment to coaching and being accountable, clients become more organized to meet their goals. In doing this, they start to allocate time to their creative needs. This often takes place to the side of their vision, while they're distracted by coaching activities. Clients are then pleasantly surprised to realize that, without trying too hard, they'd developed a regular committed timeslot that can used for future work or practice.
3. Even the most highly skilled, experienced, and talented creatives can be emotionally paralyzed with uncertainty and lack of confidence.

Self-Coaching Questions

1. If I am completely honest with myself, what practical or emotional skills do I lack to thrive in my work, and where can I get these skills? Coaching? Classes? Online courses? A mentor?
2. What is the current balance of my life? Is my creative life or career suffering because I'm not giving it enough focus? Or am I putting in too much time to my creative life or career and not being efficient or not having enough space from it?
3. Do I have old beliefs getting in my way? Do I already know what they are and need to invest time working through them? Or do I have a feeling there is a negative belief lingering and I need to invest time to pay attention to bring it in to focus?

About Sally Mazák

Sally Mazák is a creativity coach for creative professionals based in Melbourne, Australia. As a professional, she has 20 years' experience in graphic design, illustration (sallymazak.com), and writing. She has actively guided 'stuck creatives' since 2004. Sally's style of coaching is deeply reflective, informative, fun, and reinvigorating. She helps people to define or completely redefine their creative lives. In her own work, Sally tries super hard to practice what she preaches. She is also the coach for the Australia, New Zealand and UK Writers' Colleges. Contact her for individual coaching or group workshops at her website www.imagineworkshops.com.

Instagram: @sallymazak
www.sallymazak.com
www.illustratorsaustralia.com/portfolios/sally-mazak
Facebook: fb.me/sallymazakcreative
www.imagineworkshops.com

Phyllis Draws a Postcard

24

Time-Limited Creative Exercises in Session

Nancy Johnston

Before we begin a new project or return to an old one, sometimes we can feel stalled or face that symbolic block: the monumental slab of wood or granite.

Perhaps we imagine the perfect end of a project, one that seems impossible or too enormous to achieve. Perhaps other fears and life realities derail us from beginning. When everything is possible, that freedom makes every possible future error appear in front of us. Perhaps we believe the effort or process needed to make the manuscript, artwork, or essay seems like shifting a block from a pedestal.

If you're in that situation, you can begin with one word, one brush stroke, one inked letter, one stitch. You can allow yourself to freely play with and in your medium. You can explore the process of creating before immersing yourself in the project, the outline, the deadlines, and the eyes of your inner critic.

My client Phyllis wanted to talk about getting back to her writing, a cultural history project. She was passionate about reclaiming stories of disabled people who have been largely erased by history. She recently finished an honor's thesis and wanted to move forward with that work, either by pursuing a graduate thesis or by launching a mixed media art project. In the past few years, she presented her work at conferences and had even undertaken a cross-country road trip to personally connect to her project. An academic thesis or art project was attractive to her. But Phyllis saw serious roadblocks: time and financial constraints, deadlines for applications to schools and grants, and objections to the project's academic value or commercial appeal.

Phyllis had not been writing lately because she felt she needed to choose a definite trajectory for her work. When we met for a coaching session, Phyllis began talking about constraints, the pros and cons of future directions, and very little about the work itself. Listening to her describe the two options, I wondered if the future—decisions and planning—was getting in the way of being in the present, blocking her momentum to move forward.

I asked Phyllis, "What do you love about your project, no matter the audience or form it might take? What do you miss, not working on it?"

"Playing with the ideas," she said. "I enjoy exploring the research." I was struck that she was becoming more disconnected from her project and that could be complicating her development process.

"What would happen if you ignored choosing a direction for your work, for now?" I asked, "Why not try something to enjoy the creative process again? Why not just begin?" I shared the mantra of Sandra Brownlee, an artist who teaches workshops that help artists reclaim the visceral excitement of preparing to begin a project. She urges us to begin with a small step or stitch: "You have to begin. You have to begin. You have to make one row." Because Phyllis mentioned that her historical characters had few recorded words, I thought something about voicing those stories could appeal to her. In that moment, I settled on a simple exercise with pen and paper.

"Draw a small rectangle. This will be your postcard," I said. I handed her pen and blank paper. "Write a few sentences inside the postcard rectangle. In the voice of one of your characters, write to someone." I gave her three minutes to work and no other instructions.

Phyllis began immediately. I stayed silent and witnessed the process. Without encouragement, she did some freewriting, filling the rectangle with sentences. When she set down her pen and looked up, I suggested: "What could go on the flip side, the picture side?" She turned over her paper and drew another rectangle. Although she had said she wasn't a visual artist, she did not hesitate. The three-minute window was not too short. When I called time and she finished a final stroke on a wilderness scene with tiny figures. I noticed she sat more comfortably in her chair, with relaxed shoulders and body posture. She still held onto her pen, as if ready to continue. She said, "I enjoyed doing this. It isn't THE PROJECT—but it's the reason why I want to continue. I think I can try this on my own and play with more ideas."

As it turned out, Phyllis tabled the BIG decision for now. Instead, she took pleasure in diving into research, remembering her original excitement about her work. She began using freewriting postcards as a regular tool to explore new themes and ideas. She is currently chipping away at the block and the project is emerging in her hands.

The creative block—with all of our fears and anxieties associated with it—may not need to be completely toppled before we can begin. Instead, we can chip away at the block through small actions. For example, a prompt or short exercise can be a low-risk opportunity to reconnect with the pleasure of creating. As creativity coaches, we can help reduce anxiety by modeling how to begin.

In tutoring sessions or coaching sessions, I touch base first with students and artists about the creative process. If they are open to exploring in the moment, I suggest a creative or expressive prompt (rather than assigning homework). These tasks are low risk and emphasize visceral motion, such as using their hands with a pen, pencil, or working with textiles or paper. I avoid suggesting exercises that involve existential questions, ones closely related to motivation, or their project. I don't ask, for instance, what is the source of your block? Nor is it the time to suggest that they create a diorama of their ideal workspace.

You can try prompts or exercises that are short, low risk, and time limited. Lynda Barry suggests that time constraints may reduce opportunities for self-critique. After the student or artist begins, I try to stop talking and simply witness the process: no coaching, encouraging, or answering questions unless absolutely necessary. When I call time, I suggest checking in about the creative process first: what was it like to begin, to continue, to finish something new here? Regular creative practice, such as activities from Eric Maisel's *The Creativity Book*, works very well to start dissolving the block.

Learning Points

For creativity coaching and self-coaching, I try to keep a regular practice of doing and immersing that allows me to "warm up" before tackling the bigger projects. For more ideas and prompts, I recommend reading Eric Maisel's *The Creativity Book: A Year's Worth of Inspiration and Guidance* or Lynda Barry's *Syllabus* for wonderful ideas for daily practice and habits.

1. Help your client begin by thinking small. Try small steps and small stakes. Talk about a low-risk creative activity and a limited time to practice. Suggest they keep pens, pencils, and notebooks at hand for when they need them in life and, if you're a coach, keep them on hand yourself for use in session.

2. Encourage creative play and be prepared to do it in your session. You might suggest a quick warm-up exercise such as writing an over-heard dialogue, trying expressive drawing with color, or copying out a favorite poem.
3. Suggest working by hand or doing handwork when they feel blocked. Writing by hand, moving a pen on paper, or holding a brush in the hand may encourage a kind of muscle memory.

Self-Coaching Questions

1. Starting somewhere can be frightening. But one chip at the block will likely not crack you or your project in half. What is a low-risk creative activity that you've enjoyed in the past? Could you use this as a warm-up for five minutes?
2. Sometimes changing the creative mode or form we use can redirect us or bring fresh ideas to our work. Try doing five minutes of doodling, sketching, or freewriting before you look at your creative project. What is another artistic medium that attracts you, even as a novice?
3. Keeping a log or a journal of your process can supplement the plans for a large project. It might include pages of draft sketches, sample materials, ideas, or copied text. Have you used a process journal before? What kinds of things would you include in your journal to support your project?

About Nancy Johnston

Nancy Johnston is a writer, educational developer, textile artist, and writing coach living in Toronto. She teaches courses in writing and gender and disability studies at the University of Toronto Scarborough, where she is also a coordinator for writing in the disciplines. Her passions are teaching writing and textile art for expressive and restorative play.

Using the Enneagram in Creativity Coaching

25

An Example at Point Nine

Janet Johnston

On Friday mornings, at a-quarter-till 10, I light the candles on the oak table and set the bright green kettle to boil in preparation for leading a writing group. I am an affiliate of Amherst Writers and Artists and have lead writing groups since 2009.

Among the writers will be Julie, a hospice nurse in her early 60s, who has written with me for five years. Her clients no doubt notice the steady compassion and gentle interest in her blue eyes. Six months ago, she asked me to help her edit some poems and essays for her family. "That's a great idea," I said. "Have you also considered submitting for publication?"

"Several years ago, I had an editor who helped me revise some poems, but I lost interest."

I shared with Julie that, as a fellow poet, I would enjoy critiquing her work, and because I would be soon be entering a coaching program, I would appreciate the opportunity to practice coaching her toward her goals. She was delighted, and we began to meet on Wednesday afternoons.

When climbing out of a box, it helps to know how it is constructed, so I asked Julie if she would be willing to use the enneagram as part of our coaching process.

The enneagram is an elegant instrument for understanding ourselves and others. I've been studying it since 2009 and find it a precise and compassionate map for personal and spiritual growth. It's too complex to describe in this essay, but within the system, there's a personality typing element composed of nine types or points of view. Each person contains aspects of all nine, but one will be home base. After home base is identified, we can learn about our natural strengths, core beliefs, and unconscious strategies with uncanny specificity.

Julie is interested, so I ask her to take the Riso-Hudson typing test from the Enneagram Institute website. I encourage her to only choose a particular point when it truly fits her experience of herself. I also caution against going straight into reading about the lower functioning aspects of the point. The inner critic would love that; however, if we focus on the badlands, how likely are we to take the first step in our journey? We need a north star that is recognizable as particular to ourselves and inspiring. Focusing on the highest level of functioning first gives us specific positives to identify with.

Julie's test results indicate that she is in the Nine group. I begin by reviewing the basic orientation to point Nine: the experience of oneness that is natural to her. That peacefulness and time in nature are central to her well-being. How extraordinarily receptive and approachable she is so that others, even strangers, often open up to her. I add that people who identify as "Nines" value feeling peaceful and can therefore have a hard time being very visible or assertive, both of which seem to invite conflict.

Julie looks over the steam rising from her mug of tea. "I have to say, that's all true." As we continue to talk, she wonders why she hasn't done much with her writing. "Sometimes I forget how much I love it. It's like, who am I to write anyway?"

It's a great opening for looking at "sloth," which is *not laziness* but a lack of attention to the present moment. People who identify in the Nine tribe can experience an amnesia of caring, also known as acedia, sloth, or inertia. It's like a soft, heavy blanket that diffuses our caring into a fuzzy dream. Without focused caring, how do we take action?

Many of us get stuck in our creative work, but the depth of self-forgetting that can envelop a person with the Nine personality style can be profound and tragic. It stems from a belief that everyone else matters but not them. To avoid conflict, Nines have convinced themselves that they are *no one special*, and because their work doesn't matter above anyone else's, why bother? It's an unconscious ruse to remain hidden.

The dream state of not mattering can last years, even a lifetime. After the blanket of acedia is identified, the Nine can ask herself, "Do I want to remain asleep? Can I remember the energy of caring about my particular life and locate that feeling in my body?" To remember oneself is a kind of resurrection. By bringing compassionate understanding to the pain underlying inertia, we begin to release it and bring crisp attention to the moment. We can reclaim caring for things that bring us joy and return to our natural state as creators. Like all growth, it is a practice. But once the Nine awakens, she can begin to identify what ignites and fuels her passion to live and create. When we can remember the pleasure of creating, we begin to pull the fuzzy blanket of inertia off.

A Nine may have slept through much of her life, and that is a painful truth to realize. But what matters is to value what remains. And after a Nine identifies her passion, rest assured, nothing will stop her. Impassioned Nines are indomitable.

On the days before we meet, Julie sends me three poems, which I prepare to explore the following day. When she arrives, we settle in with a centering exercise that brings us into the present moment and the energy in our bodies. Then Julie chooses a poem, takes a breath, and begins to read aloud.

I hear the quavering in her voice, the care with which she has held a moment and turned it over, looking for the right words to reveal it. When she finishes reading her piece, she looks shyly into my eyes. I pick up my copy of the poem she has just read and read it aloud slowly. In this moment, a shift occurs—a capillary of self-dismissal is cauterized by the alchemy of acceptance. We both smile at the magic of this simple act. Then we move into critique—questioning word choices and syntax with focused attention. Over the months that we meet, we talk about the experience of mattering and making art. As she moves from inertia to engagement, Julie brings more enthusiasm for her work to our conversations.

I'm thrilled to witness her passion for writing come forward. Her face is more expressive and her approach to her work, less doubtful. We continue to meet, even when she is diagnosed with breast cancer. It's difficult to imagine this devoted nurse as the one needing care. I'm surprised when she wants to continue to meet during chemo.

One day Julie arrives wearing a scarf around her head. Once inside, she stands before me, removes the scarf, and looks into my eyes. She is bald. For a wordless moment we share the fear, mystery, sadness, and courage of facing mortality.

Taking Julie in, I wonder: will she survive? Did she wait too long in the sleep of inertia to bring her poems and essays to fruition? The question echoes in my own awareness. Am I bringing enough attention to my work? Eventually, this leads me to acceptance. We don't have control over how long we live, but discovering one's self as worthy of creating is a worthwhile accomplishment. "Look who's here," I say. "It's beautiful Julie."

Julie is anxious to refine her work. When her intention for a piece is strengthened, she beams with satisfaction. Her enthusiasm for crafting a chapbook for her family and friends is growing, and she is even considering submitting to some literary journals. But eventually, the chemo drains her.

"This will be our last meeting for a while," she says. "I need to put all my energy into getting stronger for surgery."

"Good plan," I say.

"I'll be back," she says, and I believe her. I've seen her awaken from the sleep of inertia. I've seen her fall in love with her creative self.

Learning Points

1. The enneagram is a sophisticated, elegant tool for personal and spiritual development.
2. It can help identify beliefs, strengths, fears, and motivations that affect creativity.
3. Even if Point Nine isn't your home base, it is an aspect of human experience. By understanding each point, we understand a little more about ourselves.

Self-Coaching Questions

The enneagram describes nine basic personality types. Although each of us has one dominant perspective, all nine domains reside within us.

1. Do you forget your passion for creating? Does forgetting feel like amnesia or a heavy sleep?
2. Do you see value in holding a false belief with compassionate awareness? Will it help you as a coach to understand that some clients may hold the belief that they are "no one special" and therefore can't see that their work matters?
3. Do you connect to the passion for creating that resides in your body, even if it's just a spark?

About Janet Johnston

Janet Johnston lives in Applegate, California. She is an affiliate of Amherst Writers and Artists and leads writing groups in Auburn, Applegate, and Grass Valley. She is a student at the Deep Coaching Institute, an enneagram-based coaching program.

How Lynn Got Her Sew-Jo Back

26

Clearing Physical and Mental Clutter to Unleash Creativity

Nadia Arbach

Lynn, a sewist, came to me with the preliminary aim of decluttering her sewing space. She told me her clutter-filled 'disaster' of a sewing room was holding her back from accomplishing her best work, and she needed some support in clearing her workspace before she could even think about setting any big creative goals.

Lynn already knew that my expertise in decluttering is an integral part of how I help clients accomplish their creative goals. She had previously worked through one of my online courses to begin clearing her creative workspace, so she was familiar with my method of examining the underlying habits that lead to clutter.

We began by taking stock of her sewing room. Lynn sent me some photos and talked me through the types of sewing she enjoyed. During our first few sessions, we pinpointed the habits that were affecting her workspace and creating the clutter that plagued her: disorganized thinking, scarcity thinking, and a less-than-clear sense of her identity as an artist.

To address the disorganized thinking, I asked Lynn to create a master list of all the sewing projects she had in progress or in mind for the future. Her lengthy list included lots of 'maybe someday' projects. I asked Lynn to rate each project on a scale of 1 to 5 according to the level of excitement she felt about it. Any projects that only rated a 1 or a 2 were to be crossed off the list, and the related materials were to be decluttered out of her sewing space. After completing the exercise, she was able to clear several projects from her list.

Lynn selected five of the remaining projects to be current projects that she would work on exclusively, without being overwhelmed by the thought of all the other projects on her master list. Because she's a prolific sewist— sometimes completing up to six projects a week—she set up her lists on a project management app called Trello, which would allow for quick and easy revision and reordering.

Next, we addressed scarcity thinking. For years, Lynn had fought, struggled, and 'gotten by,' with the feeling that these financial struggles were an unavoidable element of the mental health and disability issues she had experienced. We worked on rewriting these stories as well as the stories of hardship she had inherited from her family. I asked her to mentally flip the switch so that she was telling different stories about her life from now on. Meditations for self-compassion were already part of her repertoire, so I suggested she keep using these in challenging moments.

The scarcity thinking had found its way into Lynn's sewing room through saving items that 'might come in handy one day' and through overbuying at fabric sales. Lynn had also bartered most of her sewing work whenever she was asked to create a custom item for a client, which sometimes suited her needs but at the same time reinforced the idea that her work wasn't worth paying for. Lynn acknowledged that she was more on 'the artist side of the scale,' and her preference would be to make unique items for her own pleasure, to the most stringent standards of quality. If anyone wished to purchase these items, she would be glad—but she wouldn't be making them for the specific purpose of selling them.

This brought up another limiting self-belief related to money: "I put too much into things—they have to meet MY quality requirements. But nobody's ever going to want to pay for the quality that I want it to be."

We agreed that Lynn needed to acknowledge the value of her own work in order to believe that someone else would be willing to pay for it. Diminishing her value, bargaining, bartering, and thinking in scarcity mode were causing her to doubt her worth. I asked Lynn to think of the 10 favorite items that she had made in the past and to assign them a value directly from her instinct (even if she wasn't planning to sell them). I asked her not to think about the 'usual' price of these items, the time taken, or the value of the materials—just go from the gut and assign a price that made her happy. I encouraged her to do this from now on whenever she priced an item for sale.

When we came to Lynn's sense of identity as an artist, she acknowledged that this was the issue preventing her from clarifying any creative goals. Her self-esteem had 'taken a beating' over the past few years, during which time she had become unsure of her own likes and dislikes. However, she knew that she had made some progress in regaining her confidence and was now beginning to 'thrive instead of just survive.' She mentioned a 52-week online sewing challenge that she had taken part in the year before:

"It really helped to get me back into a routine of sewing again. There were prompts to sew a different item each week. I did make a point of sewing something each week—but I went rogue with the topic."

"How did that feel?"

"Like I was learning to trust myself again. It was so much fun and a wonderful exercise! But I consciously decided not to rejoin this year."

"Why was that?"

"I felt I didn't need that much guidance any longer."

"So, what does the next step look like now?"

"Building that trust in myself. Creating my own program of work, with permission to disregard my own rules. Examining my own body language as a clue to whether I really want to do something or not."

Lynn had reached the point of no longer needing prompts or a schedule, had begun to trust herself again, and was aware that she was now able to disregard any 'rules.' But she was still having trouble deciding which route to take. I suggested that she do some journaling on the subject of her creative dreams to see if she could unlock any ideas.

The decluttering work was continuing during these sessions, but it was progressing 'painfully slowly,' as Lynn put it. She had been trying to organize her sewing room 'like with like' (all fabrics together, all threads together, all patterns together, and so on), which is the standard setup for many sewing spaces. However, we made a breakthrough when we realized that almost every single item in the room was already earmarked in Lynn's mind for a specific use in one of her listed projects and that Lynn also had an uncanny ability to visualize the locations of all her disparate items, no matter where they were in the room. We realized that we could completely bypass 'like with like' and store the materials using a 'project-by-project' framework.

Immediately, Lynn set about organizing her sewing space on a project-by-project basis, bringing together the materials for each of the projects on her master list. She put everything she needed for a single project (fabric, thread, pattern, zips, and so on) in its separate container and stored the containers on her shelving unit, with everything ready for a project whenever it reached its turn on the current projects list.

After this breakthrough, the decluttering and organizing work went much more quickly. Lynn found that she actually enjoyed the work rather than feeling like it was a chore. She was finally operating within a framework that felt right to her.

With Lynn's first big goal of eliminating the clutter from her sewing space fully under way, we turned our attention to setting her next goal of a creative project that really stretched her limits. However, despite having followed my suggestion to engage in some journaling work around her creative goals, Lynn was still having trouble thinking of a 'big dream' project that would require her to take her creativity to the next level.

Sensing that we might do well by examining her typical pattern of working, I asked her to explore the commonalities among her past projects. The ensuing discussion unearthed five recurring elements that were incorporated into all her favorite projects. Finally seeing the connections between these projects awakened Lynn's understanding of her typical method of working, which she had never fully articulated to herself before. This gave her another unique framework within which to operate, which felt completely right to her.

Immediately, she thought of a project idea that she had mentioned just in passing in one of our first meetings. This project contained all five elements that characterized her typical way of working, but it would challenge her to expand on all five of them to a degree she had never attempted before. This would be the perfect project to pursue next, she decided, because it would raise her work to a level that she had never attained before.

Lynn's growth during our sessions together was facilitated not only by discovering two unique frameworks that worked for her but also by her willingness to face and overcome both the physical clutter and the limiting self-beliefs she had about scarcity and struggle. When we first began, she had just come out of 'survival' mode and only a few months later was ready to push her creative boundaries and self-expression in a way that she could never have foreseen.

Learning Points

1. Clutter in your workspace can drain your creative energy even if you don't realize it. Making sure your workspace is clear and ready to use is one way of setting yourself up for success in your creative practice.
2. Mental clutter can also drain your creative energy, hold you back, and keep you playing small. Paying attention to the old stories you're telling yourself will make you more aware of the negative self-talk you may be engaging in and will give you the opportunity to address it.

3. Finding a useful framework that encapsulates your method of working, outlines your way of organizing your space, or describes any other system that helps you get your creative work done will help you achieve clarity and give you inspiration for your future work.

Self-Coaching Questions

1. Is a cluttered creative workspace preventing you from doing your best work? Take a look around and see whether you're keeping items that no longer serve you. Can you let any of those things go?
2. If you find yourself reluctant to let some of your clutter go, that's actually great—it's pointing you in a direction that you need to pursue more deeply! Write a list of the five items that you just can't seem to declutter. What are they telling you? Are you keeping them out of sentimentality or nostalgia? Out of a sense of scarcity? Out of a less-than-confident sense of your identity as an artist? Whatever the reasons, exploring them further may help you realize you no longer need those items in your life. Let them go if you can!
3. Take a look at your five favorite past projects. Is there anything that ties them together? Look for commonalities or patterns in the way you work. Pinpointing these and understanding them as your 'modus operandi' means you can use them to plan future projects where you push your boundaries in one or more directions.

About Nadia Arbach

Nadia Arbach, The Creativity Coach, helps women transition their creative hobby into their creative DREAM LIFE. This might mean starting a creative business, writing the book they've been dreaming about, having their work featured in an exhibition, or otherwise moving their creative work from being on the sidelines to sitting at the very core of their life. She uses her expertise as a professional declutterer to help her clients cut through any mindset issues that are no longer serving them, let go of their old identity as a hobbyist, and step right up to going PRO! She is the author of four self-study online courses for creative women and runs a parallel business, Clear the decks!, helping creative women declutter their creative workspaces You can contact Nadia via her websites at http://nadiaarbach.com and http://clearthedecks.co.uk. You can also find her on Instagram at @nadiaarbach and on Facebook at www.facebook.com/clearthedecksUK.

The Coaching Side to Private Tutoring

Preparing the Ground for a Successful Outcome

Susanne Rieger

Maria came to me for private tutoring because she was in danger of not being promoted to the next grade, into the 10th grade, because of her bad marks in French. In addition, she was not very popular with her teachers and her classmates because she displayed some behavioral disorders, including some minor autistic tendencies. Her mother had told me that she had informed her daughter's class teacher about these disorders, but the teacher was not taking this information into account. On the contrary, the mother had the impression that she had made her daughter's situation worse by informing the teacher.

When Maria arrived at my office for her weekly coaching sessions, she was initially not open to learning at all. She wanted to talk. I could sense that she was under great pressure. I knew that it would not make sense to start teaching her French, which was the actual goal of our session. Maria had to let off steam, to vent her anger caused by a lot of things. She needed to complain about her "stupid" teachers and classmates, about the deadly boring class hours—and in general about the school as such. Evidently, there was always trouble at home, too. Her father didn't like her surfing the Internet a lot and threatened her with confiscating her computer; her mother wanted her to help in the household and expected she would at least tidy up her room. And, of course, her parents took for granted that she would be promoted into the next grade. This went without saying: this was an unspoken but clear expectation.

Since I had noticed that Maria was under great pressure, I let her complain for 5 to 10 minutes. I knew for sure that my teaching would not fall on fertile ground if I didn't grant Maria this time to let off steam. It was evident that Maria was in no condition to learn. So, I just let Maria tell me her stories. I listened carefully and signaled to her that I understood her anger and that I saw that things were not easy for her. I said things like "Mm-hm," "I see," "This was really tough for you," "This was really annoying," "And you wished they would understand you," and similar supportive responses.

This approach allowed Maria to slowly calm down and relax. I could see this in her changed body posture. First, she was sitting in a quite tense way in the chair, as if ready to jump. The more she expressed her anger, the more she could relax and lean back in the chair. Her facial expression became softer. At a certain point, she seemed to be ready to learn. She had expressed everything that she had always wanted to express. Her body and her facial expression told me when this point was reached. Her face relaxed, and she began to smile. She was also able to keep eye contact with me, to react to it, to listen to what I said, and to take in my words. A further indication was that she started to speak about some good things happening in her life, too: the cake she had made for her mother's birthday, to the joy of her mother; the moped driver's test she had passed; the pranks her little dog was playing. Now was the time when we could start to work on our ultimate goal—improving Maria's French—in a relaxed atmosphere.

We had prepared the fertile ground for success. Now I could ask Maria questions like: "How is it going in French?," "Anything new in French?," "Would you like to show it to me?," and so on, so as to make the transition to actually start learning French. Thanks to these questions, Maria began to take her French books out of her school bag. While doing so, she already told me about the subject matter in French class and where she had some problems.

To gain a good overall picture of her situation in French, I asked her to show me the texts and exercises in her textbook as well as the associated grammar. In addition, her manner of speaking provided me some information about where she had problems with French at the moment. Furthermore, I asked her to show me her homework and her class tests in case she had gotten back a test since our last meeting. Then we went through everything. We had a closer look at her mistakes. We discussed them, I gave her the missing information when required, and Maria corrected them. Maria trusted me because of my being understanding and thus could openly tell me all her problems with French. This was extremely important for real help.

After I had listened to Maria in a friendly way and obtained an overview of her problems in French, we were able to start working on them in a relaxed and focused way.

In this atmosphere founded in mutual trust, we continued to work for six months. Most of the time Maria was open to my offers and suggestions. She did the exercises in her French textbook with me supporting her. I gave her additional worksheets that I had created specifically to address her problems so that she could practice in an effective and focused way. When we met the next time, she told me how she had gotten along with French in general and with the work sheets. She told me what was difficult for her and what was easy. And the best thing about it was that Maria was promoted to the 10th grade. This was, of course, a reason to celebrate.

Learning Points

1. When supporting a client to solve a problem, it is very important to look carefully at what kind of support the client needs. It could be that the most obvious solution alone will not work because there are more aspects to consider, as in this chapter's example. If I had just taught French, I wouldn't have gotten very far because the student was not able to listen and learn French. So, my first step was to restore the student's capacity to listen and to learn.
2. In coaching it is extremely important to create a basis of trust. Then you can work together in an effective and fruitful way and reach the desired goal. Only when your clients feel seen and heard can they trust you as a coach and accept your support.
3. As a teaching coach, having a well-developed sense of empathy in addition to your specialized knowledge is essential. You have to offer your clients the space that they need for their development on the one hand and to create a clear structure and to set boundaries on the other hand.

Self-Coaching Questions

1. How can you create a friendly atmosphere of trust in your sessions so that you and your client can work together in an effective way and reach the desired goal?
2. Do you know the real cause or causes of your client's problem? What does your client need in order to be able to overcome the problem?

3. How much room do you give your clients for simply telling their story in a session? How can you interrupt your clients in a kind way without hurting them when they are speaking at length? In case you have inadvertently hurt your client, what can you do to win back possibly lost trust?

About Susanne Rieger

Susanne Rieger is a creativity coach based in Germany, working with people who seek to balance heart and mind in a full life. She uses a broad palette of tools, including deep listening, creating space, yoga nidra, focusing, non-violent communication, painting, and body movement. Susanne has a varied background as a translator, language teacher, personal coach, painter, photographer, mother, and vital human being. You can find out more about her coaching and art at www.susanne-b-rieger.com.

The Guitar or the Code

28

From Tech Day Job to Full-Time Musician

Pragati Chaudhry

"Nothing compares to the feeling when these fingertips move on the strings of the guitar," said Jane in her first session to me.

Jane loved to make music on her guitar and even went to school for music education. But she had to settle for a computer-based job in information technology in which she created codes for security applications. Her musicianship was barely able to stay alive through playing at church.

"I need to keep this job to sustain myself, but I dread waking up for coding every day. I want to play my guitar, and I am grateful to play guitar for the church orchestra, but I don't feel fulfilled."

I asked her what fulfillment would look like. She said, "It would feel like freedom; pursuing something I am passionate about." I asked her how she could get there. She said, "I need to freelance gigs and step down in my job so that it becomes part time."

"How, I asked? What do you need to do first?"

Her answer became her action steps: (1) create recordings, (2) update her website, and (3) research what gigs were possible locally.

In the next few sessions, it was exhilarating to see Jane follow her action steps, trying to establish a balance between her paying job and rekindling her passion. She started to extensively multitask with her job as well as musical gigs in the city. As challenging as the multitasking was, it led her to desire even more. "I want to find more music in my days, and I want to find myself sharing the kind of music I compose," said Jane.

Things were going well, and Jane was making tangible progress every day. But then came a day when she came to our session feeling really down, experiencing panic. "We were so little and had to sacrifice our toys and cereal for the new baby of the family. There was only so much to go around. I cannot forget that misery and have learnt from it . . . how can I give up a stable security that gives me the means to live comfortably?" she said.

The thought of resigning her job had put her into a panic. "Music feeds my soul, but would it feed my stomach? And what if I am not successful, and people don't like what I create?" She was afraid of failure, and all the old gremlins were surfacing to make her doubt her dream.

Jane had clarity about her vision and what she wanted to manifest but questioned her worth as a successful musician because of her painful past. The pain of uncertainty about the future was evident in Jane's energy. It was clear that this life transition was disorienting her. Experiencing loss of stability, loss of financial security, and loss of identity was overwhelming her. It was a very emotional session. There was grief to deal with, and it was clear that Jane needed support so that she didn't let herself be ruled by her emotions at a time when she needed to make sound, life-changing decisions.

In the next session, I suggested a creative exercise during our time together, an exercise called "two voices within." She named one voice "musician" and the other voice "wounded." I led her through a deep meditation in which she looked at her past and at how much she had accomplished in life thus far. In doing so, she was able to see that she had functioned well in spite of being wounded by her childhood. This session was incredible in unlocking some issues that had been keeping her in a limited reality. I asked Jane what success looked like to her, and she immediately replied, "Making a living with my music."

Listening to her own answers and asking herself some powerful questions, Jane was able to realize that her self-identification of 'a freelance musician' no longer served her at this point in her career. We took the time to itemize the expectations she held of herself during this transition, and she sketched out her action steps of becoming a full-time musician and earning a living through music. She was finally really embracing this reality.

In the next session, Jane came in talking about the financial part of things. She wanted to figure out where she was financially and what might be causing her to prolong her resignation from her job. We talked about that; she admitted feeling "angry" and "resentful" about her work situation. She revealed that it was hard for her to speak up to her corporate partner about leaving the start-up company that they had worked hard to create together. When I asked her why she was avoiding speaking up, she said that the thought of speaking up made her feel guilty. Jane felt a great deal of responsibility for this venture that she and her friend birthed together.

We discussed the feeling of responsibility that Jane felt towards her partner and she said, "If I leave, she has nobody; she will fall apart." As we talked further, Jane acknowledged that their work arrangement was one-sided and unequal and had been holding her back from doing anything but coding and implementation. She was always trying to be a friend and wanted to do every-thing to make the venture work. She had made a compromise with trying to keep this 'friendship' going, telling herself all along that she wouldn't be able to make it as a musician anyway. "I always thought that it was better to do this with a friend than to get a dead-end corporate job, but I realize now that I've fallen into a trap!"

Jane came to the realization that she didn't have to stay professionally tied to her partner in order to be her friend. She was ready to move on. We then took that opportunity to role play the situation of Jane speaking up to her partner. At first, she shut down. We tried it again and she was able to perse-vere. She told me what she wanted to say and then firmly but politely pushed back against the feelings of guilt she was experiencing.

The next day, Jane gave her leave notice and agreed to serve for six weeks until her friend and partner found a replacement. These six weeks were important for Jane. She itemized all that she needed to do to wrap up the job and to start her life with more income-generating opportunities in music. There was a new hope in Jane's voice now that she started walking her own path. She had been asked several times if she would teach music lessons, but the lack of time never let her explore this area. Now she could do that and started to take on students.

Jane started to enjoy the role of being a music teacher alongside compos-ing her own music. She was able to charge by the hour and was beginning to feel comfortable with the amount she was able to make financially. Bringing the focus on marketing her own music, she created a plan to reach new record producers and magazines every week. She researched the ones she wanted to talk to and persisted in following up with them after meeting them.

Over time, Jane achieved her creative dream, and not only did she experi-ence lot of fulfillment, but she also became a successful musician and started teaching music to many students. Money was never a problem, it turned out, and she created an excellent income for herself doing what she was passion-ate about.

Learning Points

1. Each one of us has our own special talents and abilities. We are not limited to only the 'safest' choices.
2. Within each moment rests the seed of creativity and choice. What can you choose in the next second?
3. We can create from a state where we are not restrained by the limitations and fears of our mind.

Self-Coaching Questions

1. How have you defined yourself? Is it possible that you are more expansive than this defined identity?
2. What are the chances that what you are creating is also creating you in this moment of time?
3. What are you gaining from procrastination? Is it an insight of some kind, or are the gremlins from the past resurfacing?

About Pragati Chaudhry

Pragati holds a degree in Fine Arts (MFA), and in teaching Fine Arts (MST) and loves leading people to a space where they stop creating from a place of struggle and start reclaiming their true creative power. She has had the privilege to work with extraordinary people from all around the world who followed their calling to connect with their creative alchemy. Trained as a creativity coach and as a life coach and having studied Trauma-Informed Expressive Arts Therapy, Pragati offers coaching and workshops for deep transformation through art and writing. She can be visited at: www.creativealchemies.com, www.pragatichaudhry.com, www.consciouscreationenergetics.com, and www.fineartheals.com.

Alison the Ambitious Academic   **29**

Managing Overwhelm and Inefficiency Caused by Competing Demands

Vinita Joseph

I call Alison on Skype, as we've scheduled and, after a moment, a smiling face appears on my laptop screen.

"Hello!" she says. "Thanks for seeing me at such short notice." She makes good eye contact and has the cheerful confidence of a game show host. I wonder what could have been so urgent.

I know from her email that she's an assistant professor at a university, and I ask her to tell me more about her situation.

"I'm at a critical point in my career," she explains. "My application for tenure—a permanent position—is due next year. To stand any chance of success, I need to finish writing my first book. The publishers have accepted my proposal, so it's simply a matter of getting on with it. Except that it doesn't feel simple, and I'm not getting on with it. And I don't know why." Her voice trails off, and she looks away from the screen.

As well as a book, the university also expects her to publish several papers in reputable journals alongside fulfilling teaching and administrative responsibilities. Her husband is a technician at the same university, and his employment is both part-time and precarious. They have twins aged four.

Alison rubs her temples as she continues. "To be honest, the workload is grueling. I'm always behind, no matter how many hours I put in. I never get enough sleep, and I'm exhausted. Last week, I caught myself snapping at the kids for being boisterous. But I can't let up. I *have* to get tenure. Our financial security depends on it."

The pressure on Alison sounds extreme, but hers is a common scenario among the academics I coach. Not all are up for tenure, but most struggle with the requirement to publish alongside teaching commitments. As Alison is experiencing, this level of stress can have a negative impact on family life.

"So, of all the competing work demands, what's the most important?' I ask. Alison responds without missing a beat, "The book."

But when we explore her daily routines, we discover that she leaves working on the book until last. More often than not, if she manages to get to it at all, she is exhausted and makes little progress. This makes the task seem even more daunting, which, in turn, adds to her reluctance to tackle it. The less she writes, the less she feels like writing. She's in a downward spiral.

In her busyness, Alison has forgotten that: *The most important thing is the most important thing* and needs to be prioritized as such. It's a simple mantra and one well worth remembering.

We end our first session with Alison setting a goal around time management. She will dedicate the three mornings in the coming week when she is not teaching to her writing. When I ask her to be more specific, she says she'll try to draft a short section. I continue to press her until she sets herself a goal to write 1,000 words of the epilogue. We agree to have two more coaching sessions and to review her position after that.

At our second session, Alison reports that she only managed to write on the first of the three mornings allocated. On the second morning, one of her children was sick, which meant she was up in the night and too tired the following morning to tackle something difficult. On the third morning, she made the mistake of checking her email account first thing and became side tracked by administrative tasks. Despite all this, she felt encouraged because she'd made more progress on the book than she had in many months, adding 500 new words to her manuscript.

I set her an exercise to list all the tasks she needed to do to complete the book and to color code the tasks in red, amber, and green depending on the level of concentration needed. This would be a working document that she could amend as the manuscript developed. With footnotes, the bibliography, and miscellaneous bits of research, she realized that there were many tasks she could work on to progress the book even if she was not feeling at her best.

We set another time-management goal for Alison not to check her email until noon on the days she planned to work on the book. Later, Alison would tell me that, simple though this was, it was one of the most useful changes to her working practices. We agreed to meet again in two weeks' time.

As soon as Alison's face appears, I can tell that something is wrong. She has dark circles under her eyes and is agitated in a way I have not seen before.

"I'm very upset," she confirms. A paper she submitted to a prestigious journal was rejected. "Since getting the email, I've done nothing but fret, and I've made myself feel so much worse," she laments.

She acknowledges that she has always taken rejection badly. "It can knock my confidence for months. I start believing that I'm an imposter, incompetent, a total failure."

We spend some time reality checking. Alison acknowledges that rejection is common in academia, particularly when you are trying to break new ground. I ask her how she would advise a colleague or one of the students she supervises in a similar situation. Her expression lightens, and her changed demeanor tells me she is tapping into a part of her that feels confident and competent. I suggest that, for our next session, she prepare a document setting out the advice she would give a colleague experiencing rejection. We are often kinder to others than we are to ourselves.

Alison decides to continue with coaching. Over the coming months, she experiences various ups and downs—which are inevitable, no matter what strategies you put in place—but by the end of the year, Alison's book is published and, the following year, she achieves tenure. Even though Alison has met the initial goals she set for herself, she continues to have monthly coaching sessions. She says they keep her on track.

Learning Points

1. Set yourself a specific writing task. Even though I do not deal with the content of my clients' work and, unlike a supervisor or mentor, usually have no expertise in their field, I often ask them to talk through their project to help them break down and clarify their writing goals.
2. Divide up the tasks you need to complete into three categories: those that need your best, most focused attention; those that require a medium level of concentration; and those that can be tackled even when you are tired or distracted. Color code them like traffic lights—red, yellow, and green. This will help you to prioritize your work and enable you to make progress on your project even when you are not at your best.
3. If dealing with a recurring and inevitable issue such as rejection, consider how you would advise someone else in your field—a colleague or supervisee—facing this same difficulty. If you wish, create a document (no more than two pages) setting out the steps that you would advise this other person to take. The next time you encounter this difficulty, reach for the document and take your own advice.

Self-Coaching Questions

1. What is the most important thing for you to achieve?
2. How can you ring fence time for the work that is most important to you? If technology has made you available 24/7, then use technology to fight back whether by means of an Internet blocker, out-of-office or research auto-responses on email accounts, and blocking out time for your writing in your diary.
3. Identify why this project matters to you. What will be the cost—emotional, financial, and psychological to you (and your family) of not completing it?

About Vinita Joseph

Vinita specializes in coaching academics and creatives. Her previous experience as a family lawyer and a long-standing mindfulness practice brings a potent combination of strategic thinking and spaciousness to her coaching. Vinita became accredited as a coach when she was doing a PhD in creative writing and identified a gap in the support provided by her university. She now uses creativity coaching to help PhD students and academics complete their research projects. Her scheme won an award for teaching innovation in 2016. A writer herself, she also works with creatives.

You can find out more about Vinita and her work at

Vinita Joseph—Coaching Solutions

www.vinitajoseph.com

Or email her at vinita@vinitajoseph.com.

Alex Markets Himself as An Artist   **30**

An Artist Learns to Believe in Himself and His Art

Niki Anandi Koulouri

Alex is 35 years old and works at a café four times a week. His salary is low but sufficient to help him pay the rent on his small house and cover his basic needs without having to ask his family for money. In his free time, he makes installations and is a painter.

He is a self-taught artist, selling his artwork to his friends and acquaintances for a small fee. His artwork is often priced only a little bit higher than the material he uses to make them with. In the past year and without any intention to do so, he has created a small clientele that contacts him and commissions artwork from him, allowing him to accumulate a certain cash flow. However, he cannot leave his steady job at the café because that salary is significant for his livelihood and offers a certain sense of financial security.

Alex lived and grew up in a small provincial town 200 miles from Athens as the third of the five children of his middle-class family. His mother and father were not educated, so they opened up the mini-market in their town that still runs today and where three of his four siblings work.

I started working with Alex one July. The first meeting was a gift from his best friend, who knew me personally. Shortly into our introduction and our first conversation, Alex told me he "did not really believe in coaching and psychotherapy," but his best friend insisted on his coming. I asked him what drove him to come.

"Just curiosity," he said at first. Then he added, "And the insistence of Peter, who said you can help me."

"Nice. How can this meeting be useful to you?"

"I would like to put my thoughts together," he replied reluctantly. He went on, "You know, I am an artist, but I cannot live on it." The he started talking about himself, his life, and his art. When he was a teenager, he used to imagine himself painting, making installations and living on it. "But my family doesn't understand any of this. You have no idea what kind of bullying I have endured from my dad and my older brother each time they saw me drawing. But I want to paint. Each time I paint or make an installation, I completely lose myself. I feel like a fish in water," he said.

He continued talking. Finally, he stopped, looked at me, and with a sigh, he said: "Now what?"

The ball was in my court. I explained to him what coaching is and what it is not, its difference from psychotherapy, and how we could work together. I asked him to state two or three goals that he would like to achieve during coaching.

The first answer that came out of Alex's mouth was "I do not know."

"All right," I answered. "If you could paint the result, what would that be?"

He paused. "I would like to put my thoughts together and do certain things."

That was our modest beginning. The session ended, and I suggested that he continue thinking about his goals between now and the next session. I gave him a page with questions that would help him think. I suggested that he paint his ideas and his thoughts if he wished. The most important thing was to work toward understanding what his goals were and how he could achieve them.

Two weeks later, Alex came to the next meeting appearing perky and in a great mood. He had made an initial plan regarding his goals. After a brief conversation, we agreed to work on the three following goals:

1. He would talk about himself and his art without feeling arrogant and be able to say that he was an artist.
2. He would learn how to sell his art and talk to his clients about pricing with ease, as if it were something normal.
3. He would have his first art exhibition, even if it was part of a collaborative project. He would make a plan about how to participate in a collaborative project: what he should do, with whom he should talk, what his obstacles were going to be, and how he could overcome them.

I started giving certain exercises to Alex and encouraged him to work at his own pace at home and then, during our meetings, to talk about them, about his thoughts, his feelings, his insights, and their impact on him. During our time together, we discovered the following:

- He had limiting beliefs regarding his ability to make art and make a living from art. These included thoughts like, "These things, like selling art regularly and for good prices, are not for people like me" and "You can only do art if you are rich and then only as a hobby."
- He engaged in intense negative self-talk about his art, criticized himself and his art, and showed no self-compassion.
- He had feelings of shame about what he did and the fear that he might be looked upon as arrogant every time he talked about his artwork.
- Each time he had to talk about his fee, he felt embarrassed, hesitated, and changed the subject.
- He felt angry at his family's response to his desire to be an artist.

Alex told me about the time that a client expressed an opinion about Alex's art with which Alex disagreed. Alex took an absolute and rigid position with the client because he was boiling inside thinking about his father's similar objections. He saw his client's interference as similar to his father's. He found that he was afraid that people were going to exploit him and that, as a result, he was bound to make wrong choices.

We worked steadily on his goal of being part of a collaborative exhibition. We created an action plan, identified his hopes and goals for such an exhibition, worked on time management and habit change, identified aspects of his routine that he wanted to do differently, named the obstacles he was bound to face and how he would meet each one, looked at what had worked in the past and what hadn't, identified what he could control and what he couldn't, and looked at the advantages and disadvantages of each choice he needed to make.

At the same time, we looked at how his art-making connected to the rest of his life and his other life purpose choices. He asked himself, and answered, the following sorts of questions:

- What impact do I want to make on the planet?
- How do I wish people to remember me?
- What are my talents, and how am I going to make the most of them and create meaning and purpose in my life?
- When can counteract the sense of meaninglessness in my life?
- Which of my values are most important to me?

We did much of this work following the A.B.C.D.E model of cognitive psychology, which describes the five stages that help us change our limiting beliefs to more supportive beliefs. Alex's journey continues to this day. He hasn't gotten into a collaborative show yet, but he has made much progress in speaking more easily about his prices, charging more for his commissions, and realizing that art really is an integral part of his vision and mission. He has accepted his talent as an artist and that he can contribute something and leave his imprint.

He has learned the importance of setting significant, clear, specific, realistic goals in alignment with his values while at the same time taking small steps daily that will lead him closer to his goals. Likewise, he now realizes that his thoughts create his feelings and influence his reality. Now he regularly engages in self-reflection and observes how his irrational thoughts hinder him and what he can do to change them from limiting to supportive.

Learning Points

1. Family dynamics matter in the lives of artist. They can get angry at customers when they are really still angry at their parents!
2. Many clients may enter coaching skeptical about whether coaching can help them. Don't let their skepticism upset you—just do the work!
3. Help clients set goals and make sure that they break down those goals into manageable smaller tasks and objectives. Help them learn to do one small step at a time.

Self-Coaching Questions

1. What do I believe about myself and my art? How does what I believe influence my actions?
2. How can I make a realistic plan to achieve my goals and train myself to stay committed to them? How can I direct my energy more efficiently to make the best use of my time?
3. How can I develop my marketing skills?

About Niki Anandi Koulouri

Niki Anandi Koulouri is a Certified Trainer and Coach with a broad portfolio of clients, including entrepreneurs, executive leaders, and artists. She is a member of the European Mentoring Coaching Council (EMCC), Creativity Coaching Association, and International Enneagram Association. As a coach, she facilitates people to use their potential, creativity, and talents; live a conscious life with meaning, purpose, and joy; and achieve their goals. Her coaching style is situational and client centric. It varies between nondirectional and co-creational depending on the situation at hand. You can find out more about Niki Anandi and her work at www.nikikoulouri.com and www.4peoplematters.com or contact her at anandi@nikikoulouri.com

"I'm Just Not Good Enough"   **31**

How to Stop the Naysaying and Fulfill Your Creative Potential

Angela Terris

Emma was a fine artist working from a small rented studio in the evenings and weekends. She worked full time at her 'day job,' which left her with little time or energy to be creative. She scarcely made money from her artwork because she felt uncomfortable asking people for payment and often gave it away for free.

Emma told me: "There is no focus in my work. I have lots of good ideas, but I am aiming to please others rather than concentrating on what I would love to do. It leaves me feeling directionless. It doesn't help that I lack the confidence to take my work to the next level and that I shy away from calling myself an artist."

Emma had contacted me after reading an article I had written about 'artists and money' and wondered if creativity coaching could help her. She wanted to build confidence in her abilities and to be 'good enough' so as to be able to call herself an artist. She added that her WOW wish was to have a bigger studio.

In our first coaching session, I asked Emma, "What would help you feel more confident in your artwork?" and "What would need to happen for you to be braver in sharing your work?" We discussed ideas, and Emma identified three areas she wanted to work on that would help her have the much-needed confidence boost she craved. These were:

1. To increase her skills so that she felt more like a professional
2. To get more focused on what she produced and to create one complete collection of artwork to sell
3. To have a realistic long-term plan in place to reduce her 'day job' hours and to have more time in her studio

Emma felt that these were realistic goals and became excited about moving forward, which she hadn't done in a long time. Part of our working together was to address the obstacles and challenges that were getting in Emma's way of her dream of being a productive, selling artist. These challenges included all of the following ones:

1. She felt restricted by her studio size and unable to create the artwork she wanted to create in so small a space.

2. There was a discrepancy between how much productive time she thought was available to her compared to how much time she really had.

3. Her fear of failure kept her in her comfort zone, leading to procrastination in moving forward.

4. Her devaluing her artwork made her doubt whether anyone else would want to buy it.

5. Comparing herself with other artists further along on their career paths left her feeling not good enough.

Quite a lot there. It was understandable that Emma felt stuck and unmotivated. What worked in Emma's favor was her hope that things could get better and the determination to start moving toward what she wanted.

Part of my role as a coach was to help Emma unravel these problems so that she could address them one at a time, helping to reduce overwhelm and get a better picture of how things actually were. Together we agreed to a three-month coaching period, including six online video sessions and email support in between the calls, to help her find her feet again.

During the online calls, we would look at each goal to see what the next steps were, breaking them down into smaller, realistic actions doable in the time available to her. It allowed space for her to purely reflect on her creative practice, giving it the focus and attention it needed in order to thrive.

In the weekly email check-ins, Emma was able to reflect on her progress. Was she still just thinking about things, or was she putting action behind her words, no matter how small that action might be? It helped her to keep on track, recognize any progress that she made, and discuss any concerns that might have arisen. In this way, she had someone to celebrate her successes, no matter how small or big they were.

Emma explained, "I was able to explore my mistakes and successes without freaking out. I took a step back to be more objective about what I was doing and being honest about what was working and what wasn't working. It let me rebuild something far more 'me' and with some real enthusiasm. The whole process enabled me to set goals and thoughts to paper and focus on what to do next."

The primary challenge for me was helping Emma deal with all the ideas that she was generating. Her inspiration freely flowed, making it difficult for her to concentrate as her grasshopper mind jumped from idea to idea. It was as if a green light had been switched on and Emma had her foot hard down on the gas pedal. I needed to put the brakes on a little so as to slow her down and keep her focused. I was worried that this slowing down might take the joy out of the process for her, but I thought it necessary. I didn't want to get carried away with her enthusiasm and forget my role, which was essentially to keep asking, "Is this new idea moving you toward where you want to go or away from it?"

At the end of our time working together, I remarked to Emma, "You've grown in confidence; it comes shining through now when you talk about yourself as an artist. You seem more comfortable showing people your work and talking proudly about it. You've been working hard on building your skills, researching new studio spaces and especially focusing on one area of your artwork to create a cohesive collection."

Her remaining challenges were still the time restrictions imposed by her day job, the too-small studio space, and a lack of assurance about selling her artwork. But she came away from the coaching feeling that her confidence was building a little each week. She was more comfortable with her skills and more at ease calling herself an artist. She found that having had someone to talk to who was creative and who understood where she was coming from encouraging and supportive. Her final words were, "I now have a clearer focus on what I want to achieve, how to go about achieving it, and a renewed commitment to make it happen."

Learning Points

1.   No matter how much time you have available during the week, some progress can always be made. Work with the time you have available. It can be helpful to double the time you think something will take, so as to feel successful when you get it done 'early,' or break tasks into smaller bite-sized bits. Cut yourself some slack and be kind to yourself: you're not a robot.
2.   Creating more and more artwork can be another form of procrastination. It can be putting off finding buyers for your current work and

represent the fear you have of taking those first steps of selling your work. Ask yourself, "What artwork do I already have that is ready to go but that I'm holding back because I think it's not good enough yet?" What little things do you need to do in order for it to be ready to go? Make space in your calendar and do what you need to do before creating too many more pieces.

3. Remember that comparing yourself with others can be a sign that you doubt your abilities and the quality of your work. Build self-belief by focusing on improving yourself and by not comparing yourself to others. We all have different strengths: find yours and play to them. What your audience wants is more of you, not a watered-down version of someone else. Be proud of what you create, and others will follow your lead.

Self-Coaching Questions

1. If you could buy yourself a bit of confidence, what would that be? Here's a quick visualization to try. Close your eyes and visualize yourself going into 'The Confidence Shop' and asking the shop assistant, "I would like to buy some confidence, please." Be patient and let the image pop into your mind. What is handed to you? Alternatively, look around you. What catches your eye? What meaning does this have for you, and what is your intuition telling you is needed to upgrade your confidence?

2. What would you be, do, or have if you didn't have those limiting beliefs? Some limiting thoughts are it's not good enough yet, I might fail, my work will be rejected, and something bad might happen. What are yours? Keep a notebook near you and write down what automatically pops into your head, especially when you are working. Ask yourself, "Are these thoughts 100% true?"

3. What do you need to let go off to be or feel more confidently creative? Often, we think that we need more off something in order to be braver. But sometimes we need less: less putting ourselves down, less procrastination, less perfectionism, less buying new materials we don't need. Create a 'stop doing' list and regularly check that you're not falling back into old habits.

About Angela Terris

Angela Terris is an artist, writer, and creative coach with a background in creative business, nonprofit art organizations, and psychology. She now draws on her experience and knowledge to coach creatives to be bolder and braver in their creative choices. She works mainly with individuals, creative businesses, and organizations to develop calm, clear confidence in fulfilling their creative potential. Angela trained at Chelsea School of Art in London and set up her first creative business at the age of 22. She is best known for her book illustration, uplifting paintings and passion for supporting creatives.

Website: www.angelaterris.com

Instagram: @angelaterris

Burning Down the House

32

One Writer Rewrites Her Book From Scratch

April Bosshard

Lily, a talented writer in her late 30s, approached me for help to finish a novel she'd been working on for nearly 20 years. She'd carried it through an MFA program, classes, conferences, and several writing groups. She'd conscientiously revised sections based on peer and instructor input, including some treasured responses from well-established authors.

"I have a lot of material," she told me. "Some of it needs work, but I really like certain parts."

"Does it have a beginning, middle, and end?"

"Too many beginnings," she said, sighing. Then, with a voice full of trepidation and hope, she added, "I've been working on it *so* long. I *need* to finish it."

It turned out that Lily had a digital closet of mismatched pieces that she wanted desperately to coalesce into a novel. I sensed that hidden within the folds of all that material lurked many one-of-a-kind gems. But how were we going to sort through it all?

Digging deeper, I learned that the story had morphed and evolved over time. Certain characters had come and gone. The main character had started out as an adult and then turned into a 14-year-old. At one point, the story had been told in the voices of two sisters. Lily thought it could be a memoir because many situations were based on real life experiences, but it might be better as fiction, so she could have more freedom to take the story in different directions. It was clear that she had many story lines woven into one, and some key decisions would have to be made to allow her to move forward with *one* story.

"Which parts of the story are most important to you?" I asked. We discussed this over several calls until we'd identified the story she wanted to tell *now*. Then we focused on story structure for longer narratives such as novels and memoirs. This was an eye-opening experience for her. "Why didn't I learn any of this in my MFA program?" she lamented.

During our calls, I encouraged her to make choices that could help her create a solid middle and a well-crafted end. A big part of the writer's job is to decide what to leave in and what to leave out. These choices can be challenging and anxiety provoking, and there are myriad ways to avoid this essential writer's task. Over time Lily had found most of them, thereby sidestepping the novelist's real calling—to make one choice at a time and to do it over and over again.

We nailed down the new story line, its plot points, primary characters, point of view, and the main character's emotional arc. Lily began to feel the exhilaration of clarity even while lamenting the loss of ideas she'd had to eliminate. But clarity gave rise to confidence, and she felt more hopeful than ever that she could complete her novel.

In a way, the length of time she'd worked on the story was a good thing— she knew her story so well—but it was also an impediment because her attachment to what she'd already written over many years could get in the way of finishing the novel she was capable of writing now. So, I asked her to consider something pretty radical.

"I want you to think about writing this story from scratch, starting from page one."

She balked. "But I have all these pages. All this *work*." She argued that if she just organized it, a novel would surely reveal itself. But I wasn't so sure. If she hadn't found it already, I worried that she'd continue to get lost in the material.

I hadn't made my suggestion lightly. I knew it would be a challenge for her, but I sensed a potential breakthrough on the other side.

"Imagine that you've come home one day, and your house is on fire. Your writing was in the house. The only copy. What would you do? Would you want to write it over again?"

She said yes, and by now, she trusted that I had her best interests at heart, so she was willing to consider my case.

"Your story is fresh in your mind from our structure work. It's almost a new thing because it's so clear and alive now. I think going back to the old material is going to bog down your process, and your purpose, which is to finish this time."

She was daunted by the proposed task and still very attached to the old work.

"Let's try it for a while," I said. "The old work hasn't really burned up. It's still there. We're just going to put it aside temporarily. You can go back to it. But let's try this new way for *now*."

She decided to go along with my plan. So, I drew up a writing calendar based on the amount of writing she knew she could accomplish in a day. Then Lily proceeded with a new draft, writing one scene at a time. It was hard at first, but I reminded her that momentum would build as she settled into the process. And that's what began to happen.

A few weeks in, she said, "I've already written the scene I'm working on. The original version was good. Can't I just cut and paste it in?"

"Do you remember what happens in the scene?"

Hesitantly, she said, "Yes."

"Try writing it again from memory without looking at the other version. It's important that you don't derail the momentum you've worked so hard to get rolling."

"But what if the other version is better?"

"Don't let that stop you from writing something good now. It doesn't have to be great—great is for revisions; good enough is for drafts. Right now, you want to stay in the flow. Allow the previous scene you just wrote to lead into this one. Later, during revision, you can compare the two versions and choose the best one."

Somewhat appeased by my suggestion, she agreed to resist looking back.

Eventually, she got through that scene and continued to move forward at a steady rate. Momentum carried her, the story's vitality enlivened her, and she felt the characters taking on lives of their own.

"It's different from what I thought it would be. I'm learning more about the characters. Some new things are happening that really fit the story. I'm just trying to keep up now!"

This was a good sign, a sign of a writer being in flow with the story's unfolding rather than gathering and cobbling disparate pieces into a form. This process can be a viable option for some writers, but it hadn't worked for Lily.

As she wrote, she kept wanting to go back to the old material, but she wrote to me first, confessed her temptations, and I said there would be time for that *after* the drafting process carried her from the beginning to the end of the story.

"Once the story is complete, the part of the mind that sifts and assesses can be engaged—but that part interferes with the drafting process and should be set aside until the whole story, however imperfect, is done."

The months passed, and life threw up some difficult challenges for Lily and her family—job changes, selling her house and moving, a major lifestyle change, and a relative's multiple surgeries. Despite delays and setbacks, she kept returning to the drafting process.

Eighteen months later, she wrote to tell me something pretty amazing: "I just wrote my last scene."

I was thrilled and told her so.

She said, "As I wrote it, I got impatient and very scared, and I was surprised too, because right up until the end, the characters did things I didn't expect but things that made the story better."

"You did it, Lily! You wrote your novel from beginning to end."

"I did, didn't I?" She laughed. "It only took me 20 years!"

"Actually, it didn't. Remember? I asked you to start from scratch. You wrote this draft in 18 months."

She let that sink in. "It's true. I did." I could hear both surprise and pride in her voice.

Lily is now at work revising her novel. She expects it to take about six months.

Learning Points

1. Long-running projects can accumulate much more material than can be used in a final version. Writers must be willing to choose the story they want to write *now*.
2. There is a phrase in writing parlance that says, "Kill your darlings," which means that sometimes writers have to let go of what they think is good in favor of what truly serves the story. This is true of process too.
3. Building momentum is essential when drafting a novel, but too many writers start revising before they've completed a first draft, which results in far too many unfinished novels. Revision can, and will, come later.

Self-Coaching Questions

1. Have you been working on a project over a long period of time? Do you need to step back to assess whether you're writing more than one story?
2. Are you tempted to revise your unfinished work before it's done? Ask yourself if this is a way to avoid pushing toward a finish line.
3. What would you do if you lost your only draft of a cherished project? Would you be willing to create it again from scratch?

About April Bosshard

April is a creativity and story coach who works with writers around the world. Her keen awareness of story principles and deep understanding of the writer's craft sheds light on many of the complex issues writers face when it comes to story development and sticking to the writing process. You can find her at www.deepstorydesign.com.

Wooing the Muse With Wellness

33

How a Foundation of Health and Well-Being Can Spark New Creative Energy

Danielle Raine

In a happy stroke of beginner's luck, my very first client turned out to be one of my favorites. Sara, a writer, hired me as her coach because she was struggling with that tricky second book. She felt stuck and frustrated that she couldn't tap into the creativity that she knew was in her.

So, when she saw in my newsletter that I was launching a six-week creativity coaching program called The Muse Spa, she immediately signed up. This was my first offering as a newly qualified coach, and it was based on a 'creative wellness' approach I'd been developing, incorporating my lifelong studies into health and wellness practices with my recent creativity coach training.

I'd been experimenting with the link between our energy levels and our creativity, and I felt that this holistic approach was where I had the most to offer clients. Although Sara had never hired a coach before, she told me that the idea of 'wooing her muse with wellness' intrigued her and inspired her to just go for it.

She'd reached a place in her life where she was craving better health and more creativity, and she felt ready to devote some quality attention to both. And as a new coach, I felt that the coaching angels had delivered the perfect first client.

Sara was excited to begin. She was clear on what her blocks were, and she also had a lovely openness to this new experience. I was equally excited to begin our work together and grateful to be launching my coaching work with such a kind, inspiring kindred creative spirit.

I had chosen to coach via email and the process began with a questionnaire ebook called *The You Review*. It contained just five questions but included space and prompts for clients to share as much or as little as they felt comfortable sharing. Lucky for me, Sara was happy to really dive deep into these questions, revealing insights that helped me a great deal during our work over the coming weeks.

The questionnaire proved to be a valuable reference tool to support my coaching—a kind of blueprint of Sara's creative life. I was also touched that she had trusted me so much with her inner thoughts and feelings. After reviewing her questionnaire and a flurry of clarifying emails, I began creating Sara's first customized workbook.

Sara had identified her main challenges as consistency and follow-through, which she felt stemmed from issues related to time and energy. We agreed to tackle the energy issue first, with a view to setting a strong foundation for more focused writing goals in future weeks.

In an ideal world, we would have begun by building a strong foundation of quality sleep, but Sara was responsible for the care of an elderly relative, which meant she was up frequently during the night. So, I designed her first workbooks to support her energy in other areas. We began exploring upgrades and simple improvements in the areas of diet and nutrition, the home environment, exercise, and stress levels.

Even though this work didn't resolve her lack of sleep, it did kickstart a new vitality that began to bubble over into her creative life. From the start, Sara was highly coachable and embraced all the action steps and suggestions with enthusiasm. Following the coaching, she began to take better care of her physical wellness and made small changes in her lifestyle to reduce stress.

She also decluttered her home and turned a bedroom into a cozy-but-inviting writing room. These efforts began stirring up even more enthusiasm for her writing and gradually sparked the creative energy she had felt was missing. After two weeks of addressing her basic energy levels, I began receiving excited emails from Sara, sharing how she'd been spending more and more time in her writing room, enjoying some impromptu writing and book-planning sessions.

It seemed that all it took to reignite Sara's creative spark was a little attention and self-care. Our next focus was on how to nurture this newly inspired energy. Even though Sara had a clear goal in mind—the first draft of her next book—we agreed that for a little while longer, the only requirement would be *create as inspired*.

"Fun is my compass!" proved to be an effective motto to help her tap into the joy of writing and warm up her creative muscles. As a new coach, I was especially delighted with this approach because part of my vision had been to not only help clients find more joy and flow in their creative process but to also enjoy the actual coaching experience as well.

Sara was truly relishing her new relationship with her creative spark—or, as we called it, her muse—so we built in some space and time for them to get reacquainted, to simply rekindle the spark that had been missing. This freedom to create as and when inspired seemed to liberate Sara's muse. We hadn't set any word count goals or session plans, yet the less she demanded from her creativity, the more inspired, energized, and eager she was to write.

She began thinking up scenes and stories as she went about her daily life, new ideas for themes that excited her and had her rushing back to her writing room to scribble them down. Rebooting Sara's energy seemed to strike a rich vein of inspiration that was responding eagerly to the renewed attention. She was also enjoying a range of lovely ripple effects from this new creative energy: finding more pleasure in her home, happier relationships, and even noticing more synchronicities, things just working out well, all by themselves.

Sara seemed to be off and running, feeling inspired, full of ideas, writing almost daily, and truly enjoying her creativity again. Then, after four weeks of diligently completing her workbooks, a new resistance began to appear. The gaps between emails increased, and after one of my routine check-ins, Sara confessed that she just couldn't get into her latest workbooks.

I learned that despite her enjoyment of the program, real life had intervened and ushered in a particularly turbulent time, both at work and at home. However, she did feel encouraged that she was honoring her well-being and trusting her decision to not force the work. She planned to leave the workbooks for a while and revisit them when life had calmed down a bit.

Luckily, the resistance was limited to the workbooks, and Sara was still enjoying lots of creative energy and inspiration for her book, writing regularly and making steady progress with her first draft. We agreed to trust her intuition and simply stick with what was working, namely the freedom to create as inspired. Five days later, Sara emailed with a creative victory: the announcement that she had a completed section of the book!

Her instinct to relax and trust, to allow herself the freedom to follow her rhythms, appeared to be a winning formula for both creativity *and* productivity. And the workbooks she'd been resisting, feeling intuitively that the timing wasn't right, she later revisited and completed with ease and a sense of perfect timing.

By the end of our work together and despite some periods of resistance, Sara felt she had achieved her main intentions, namely, to rediscover her creativity and make real progress with her book. Even though there was still work to be done in completing her first draft, she told me she was "making consistent quality progress." And as happy as we both were with the productive results, we felt that her inner shifts were possibly the most beneficial.

I knew the techniques she'd learned would enable her to coach herself through future creative challenges. Sara felt inspired and empowered by her new ability to tune into her intuition and trust her creative instincts. She had let go of some of the anxiety and perfectionism that had previously held her back, adopting a lighter, freer approach and being kinder to herself.

She felt more playful with her creativity, eager and excited to write, and she felt that she was making progress *and* enjoying the journey. And Sara's new creative energy sparked ripple effects across her whole life that she believed would develop and increase over time. In one of our final check-ins, she told me, "The creativity continues to flow in so many areas. . . ."

As my first experience of coaching, I was equally excited for her and even more convinced of the power of creativity to bring the fun and magic back to life.

Learning Points

1. We are holistic beings, so improvements in any area can have beneficial ripple effects across our whole life.
2. Creativity is energy. Our wellness and energy levels can greatly influence our creativity and our access to inspiration.
3. Creative expression can enhance our enjoyment and quality of life, regardless of the end results.

Self-Coaching Questions

1. In what areas can you make some simple improvements to your health and energy levels?
2. Is there an opportunity to be playful and 'follow the fun' in your creative work?
3. Can you practice trusting and following your own creative instinct to build a stronger faith in your inner voice and intuition and your connection to your muse?

About Danielle Raine

Danielle Raine is a writer, designer, and creativity coach. She has been a creative professional and student of the creative process for over 20 years. She began her creativity coach training about five years ago and soon began coaching creative clients via email. In addition to the coaching work, her private studies of the creative process and creative living have deepened in recent years, resulting in a range of support services for creatives, including a blog, quiz, ebooks, and online courses. She is currently working on her next book exploring the link between creativity and wellness.

Website: danielleraine.com

Instagram: @danielleraine123

Working With What Is   **34**

Committing to Creative Work While Facing Obligations

Regina de Búrca

Some men, when they hit a certain age, have affairs; others buy sports cars, and still others return to college to embark on an MFA. "I hope I won't be like Frank the Tank," Guy said jokingly at the beginning of our first session, referencing Will Ferrell's hapless mature student character in the movie *Old School*.

"Hmm," I commented, noncommittedly. A part-time (not by choice) writer myself, I knew how precarious the business was and how few guarantees there were, even with an accomplished master's program on your curriculum vitae. How, 10 years after earning my own MFA, most of my peers still hadn't paid off their student loans. How only one out of 70 students who graduated in my year had been able to make a living from writing full time in the intervening years.

My challenge was to dance a fine line between managing Guy's expectations while encouraging his writing. My aim was to work with him to come up with a plan to get him where he really needed to be—not where he thought he wanted to be.

Guy and I then spent some time piecing together the broader picture. He told me how little spare time he had to write. How his stories always took a back seat to family and work commitments. How his writing was suffering from the daily grind. How he couldn't remember the last time he did something just for him. A seasoned marketing manager, Guy felt unfulfilled in and drained by his work.

"Your daily writing time can be just for you," I suggested. His wife was self-employed and home based, while his children—now 10 and 8—had their own routines, affording him the opportunity to get up earlier and avail himself of a 'golden hour' when he would have space and quiet before the rest of his family woke up.

He agreed that this hour first thing in the morning could benefit him. "I just can't wait to study full time, though. My job brings me down with the pettiness and politics. I hate how the guys at the top pile the pressure on while cutting resources to the bone. At my level, I am expected to work more and more for less. I can't wait to leave the game. This pressure is drying up my creativity."

"What is it about the pressure that is affecting your writing?" I asked.

"Just the crushing responsibility. The constant fire fighting. It's so stressful facing all these problems day after day."

Skirting around the solution I hoped Guy would become aware of and volunteer on his own, I slightly changed direction. "How will you afford the program?" I asked.

He shifted in his chair, uncomfortably. "My wife and I have agreed to remortgage the house."

Not wanting to act the heavy and scare him off by stating the obvious, I didn't mention the unstable Irish housing market, varying interest rates, or the possible impact of Brexit on Ireland; I wanted him to consider the impact of these possible risks on his own. "Are there a lot of jobs in your field?"

"Not really. Maturity isn't much of an asset. My younger colleagues don't get it. Even though they are bearing the brunt of unfair working conditions and job shortages, they buy in to the system with surprising enthusiasm. I'm noticing a trend where senior management hire younger people for shorter term contracts so they have less of an obligation to provide benefits. It's also easier for a company to get rid of an employee when they have less of an employment history. But it's the younger employees who won't challenge management and who tow the company line without question."

He still had not quite arrived at the mindset I was steering him toward. "What is the plan for after the MFA?"

"Get published, I guess," he beamed.

"Sometimes it's helpful to devise other goals as well for an MFA, ones that are more directly in your control."

"Like what?" he asked.

"Like being able to write certain story elements much better than before— or even being able to tackle a difficult piece of writing that you normally would have shied away from. Or building your network of other writers. Goals like reading more widely or sharpening your critical theory skills. Or making new friends."

"That sounds good," he said, nodding his head.

It was time to join the dots. "Because, as I'm sure anyone in the industry will tell you, the average Irish book deal is around 1,000 to 1,500 Euros for a 70,000-word novel."

"That's not very much at all," he said. "Not for that much work that takes that long. It wouldn't even cover the fees of one semester." He frowned.

"So, I think it makes sense that we focus on the nonmonetary aspects of participating in the program. Committing to your craft is an extremely worthy pursuit—and not everything is about money—but it might be wise to balance that writing commitment with other obligations."

"That does makes sense. Money worries down the line would be stressful," he admitted, his brow wrinkling.

I nodded. "So, what are your new goals for this course in light of this discussion?"

"Hone my craft. Build my network. I'm not sure about the making friends bit; in my experience, younger people don't really get it." His posture had sagged, and his voice lowered.

I looked at the clock on the shelf behind him. We had 10 minutes left—time to lift the energy and help him refocus and build his motivation back up. "There's always the part-time option," I suggested. We didn't have enough time to circle around possibilities any longer. "That way, your peers would likely have similar circumstances and responsibilities to yours. Whereas if you go with the full-time option, you will likely be surrounded by younger people, who you believe might not be on the same wavelength as you."

"And there would be less financial pressure in the long run," Guy said, finishing my line of thought.

Bingo.

I smiled. "After all, you are dedicated to being a writer for the rest of your life; it's not a short-term process. The MFA program isn't like an MBA; it's not so much about the qualification as the journey. So, there's no rush. Taking two years to complete the program instead of one could really help you reach your goals of honing your craft and building your network. The support of your fellow students will increase over time as you get to know each other better."

"That sounds much better. I'll submit the part-time application tonight. This feels better; actually, I'm relieved. I didn't realize that I wasn't completely behind this choice until now."

"After all—even Frank the Tank had to pay for beer," I noted with a smile, before wrapping up our session.

Guy did complete his part-time MFA while working full time. A regular salary meant he could buy books on the course's recommended reading list, attend supplementary courses and retreats, and get more creative coaching sessions. His company offered study leave, which he was in a position to avail himself of. Having time to explore different modes of writing, six months after graduating, he published a collection of poetry.

During his MFA, he gained transferrable writing skills that led to a promotion at work. Now a bid writer for his company, he enjoys his work more and is in a more secure role as it generates revenue directly. But more important for Guy, his writing skills are often called on for employee well-being initiatives such as diversity and inclusion policy writing, which enables Guy to live his values in a corporate setting—while writing.

Learning Points

1. Follow your bliss . . . but be prepared as you do so.
2. Make sure you're not swapping one set of problems for another; when making a big life change like Guy did, make use of tools like pros and cons lists and create SMART goals.
3. Creatives create. There is no substitute for a daily routine. Handing over responsibility for this daily practice to take part in a program won't do the work for you or make establishing a creative practice easier, unfortunately.

Self-Coaching Questions

1. What would happen if you focused on where you want to be instead of where you don't want to be?
2. What nonmonetary goals can you set for your creative work?
3. Are there ways to incorporate your creativity and values into your day job?

About Regina de Búrca

Regina de Búrca grew up in the west of Ireland surrounded by rare books and an eccentric breed of book collectors. Her parents encouraged her to tell stories, thanks to the catalogue of half-truths that she had gathered by the age of six. They believed she had taken after her great grandfather, whose only redeeming quality was his ability to tell a good yarn. Regina wrote her first book aged seven about a talking strawberry named Willis after a character in the TV show *Diff'rent Strokes*" The jury is still out on whether she's a hopeless case or not.

Refilling the Creative Well

35

Finding Voice and Flow Through Writing and Journaling

Jackee Holder

Monica contacted me for coaching supervision after having read an article about my work in a professional coaching journal here in the United Kingdom. Together we agreed that our work together would combine the creative aspects of coaching and coaching supervision to focus on the client's goal of growing and developing her creative practice. In there was a deep longing to write, to find her voice as a writer, and to share her writing publicly on social media and in print magazines.

We hit it off immediately on our chemistry call. On reflection, I realized that we shared many parallels in our personal and professional lives. We both worked corporately as leadership coaches, we were both in training as therapists (Monica was a year ahead of me), and we both had one daughter. Relationshipwise, Monica was at the tail end of becoming divorced, and I found myself in the same position almost a year and a half later.

In my mind, every client is a gift showing up as both student and a teacher. The mirror held up to me in the coaching sessions supporting Monica's creative process was and continues to be a valuable teaching and reflection into my own creative process. I learn as much about my own creative process through the work with Monica as I believe she did about the potential of her own creative resourcefulness.

Integral to our work was my willingness to be transparent about my own creative process as well as making space to share aspects of my cultural identity as a woman of color as it impacted the different perspectives I was able to bring to our work together.

I am of African Caribbean heritage, first generation born in the United Kingdom, and my client is white of English heritage, also born in the United Kingdom. Speaking openly to our cultural identities generated space for authenticity and honesty in our coaching sessions that deepened the possibility for transformational shifts in the work over the course of two and a half years.

We began our work by establishing the need for Monica to anchor a regular writing practice into her everyday routines. So often individuals come to coaching with a desire to write but with little evidence of establishing writing as a regular practice. From the very first coaching session, I invited Monica to engage in a series of free-writing and themed writing exercises as a way of warming up her writing muscles. At the same time, the immediacy of the writing practice began a drip feed of connecting her with a toolkit of accessible writing prompts that would help to seed a daily writing practice outside of the sessions.

It was not long before Monica's journal became a constant companion in her daily life. Setting it in the context of a reflective learning journal gave Monica permission to use her journaling in an organic way in between our sessions. This practice of coaching individuals to adopt their 'own work' in between sessions provides a vital link between the coaching sessions and the creative practice in the real world.

Soon Monica found herself becoming more observant of the world around her, and like a camera, her journal captured her observations in writing. This slow-hand form of analogue notation proved exceptionally rich for Monica's creative journey. Very quickly, Monica found herself pulling out her journal as she waited in the waiting room at the doctor's office, in empty time before a meeting, or during her commute from home into the city. With no limits, she began filling her journal with personal reflections and observations, quotes, and links to different aspects of her work.

From the journaling, Monica reconnected with the environment around her. Self-care is essential to the creative journey, and a combination of journaling and reflective practice saw Monica increase her exploration of time outdoors in the form of what the creativity author Julia Cameron named as artist dates. Artist dates are designed to lubricate your inner creative and need to be done alone to gain the full benefits. Needing very little encouragement from me, Monica found herself inspired to take regular walks among the green spaces and woodlands of the part of the U.K. countryside where she lives and doing these alone. Walking became a companion to her journaling.

As the winter months passed and the sunshine became more vibrant, we decided to schedule our next coaching session outdoors. London is a city bursting to the seams with green spaces, so we decided on a visit to Kew Gardens, a green oasis in the city's west side. Our chosen day was hot and humid, perfect weather for this nature-inspired coaching session. We met in one of Kew's cafe's and spoke for 30 minutes, clarifying the focus of the session and what Monica wanted to achieve during her time.

Monica was bursting with energy at the hour and a half she would get to spend in the gardens of Kew. She described feeling as if her inner child was being let out to play. We contracted for an hour of musing, doing whatever she wanted in the space, and agreed to meet back at the cafe in one hour's time. So off I went walking through the grounds, stopping to connect with the rich collection of trees, when I unexpectedly caught sight of Monica sitting under the shade of a huge pine tree with her notebook in hand, writing away. She looked at home. I sat under the canopy of a giant plane tree close by whose leaves dangled like huge hands in the frail breeze. Suddenly I felt the urge to pluck off one of the huge hand like floating leaves from a low-lying branch. Next thing I knew I was writing words directly onto the succulent green leaf as if it were a blank page in my notebook. This spontaneous practice gave me an idea of a closing ritual to share with Monica as a way of ending her session in nature.

I invited her to pick a leaf from the same tree and to write down the words of all the things she was willing to let go off so she could focus on her creative goals for the future. Monica described her time sitting under the tree as magical, showing me several of the tree sketches she had drawn during her time, including the image that became a catalyst for the birth of her newsletter, a writing project she had wanted to get off the ground for some time. It is often in the space away from work and the routines of daily life that your creative ideas flourish. 'The Inspiration Tree' image created that day by Monica in Kew Gardens was featured in the launch of her first monthly newsletter.

Our work then focused around Monica cultivating her writing voice and strengthening her writing and creative practice. We started off with her trying out in-the-moment writing practices. This helped to soothe any anxieties Monica had about what she could write about and whether her writing was good enough. As a creativity coach, I aim to get as much writing done in these early face-to-face sessions as talk about writing. My experience is that the way through is to write or create in the moment.

Monica arrived telling herself that she did not know what to write about and not feeling confident about her writing. The in-the-moment writing practice allowed Monica to experience for herself how she could write past her fears and the voice of her inner critics and still get to the other side, this time with words solidly planted on the page, words that did not need to be perfect or even make sense. This marked a shift; in the past, the fear would have meant paralysis.

Another area that was central to our work together was the client's inner critic. One area we focused on was the way in which her inner critic would want to quickly move onto her next goal or achievement at the expense of really taking time to appreciate what had just been achieved. So, despite a year of sending out a monthly newsletter and having written a year's worth of newsletters for the new year, she found that her inner critic was still subtly diminishing the fullness of her achievement. I was able to reflect this back to Monica and to help her see why celebrating her achievements was crucial in ensuring that she nourished her own self-worth.

Looking back, I see how far Monica has traveled. It is like looking at a colorful quilt full of rich, textured, and layered vibrant colors and images. The work of the creative coach offers a lens into the inner life of the client in ways that are transformative and profound. This is transpersonal work and in many ways sacred work.

Learning Points

1. Include the practice of Reflect Writes (Adams, 2016). Reflect Writes distill the learning and insights from processes and experiences. A short feedback Reflect Write after either a writing session or a conversation can heighten learning.
2. It is important to help creatives identify and embrace smaller steps of progress, not as inconsequential bits but as building blocks moving them closer to the bigger picture.
3. Many blocks in the creative process are emotional or psychological. Creative coaches need to be psychologically minded so they can better support individuals with ways and methods to effectively navigate and dissolve psychological blocks and barriers.

Self-Coaching Questions

For Coaches:

1. What have I learnt about my own creative journey that I could embed into my own creative practice?

2. What do I appreciate my client for teaching or making me more aware of?
3. Where was I challenged in our work together, and how might I develop this as a learning point in future creative work?

For Creatives:

1. When am I at my most creative?
2. What factors contribute to me holding creative space?
3. What small step or action can I take to give voice, shape or form to my untold story today?

About Jackee Holder

London born and raised, Jackee loves the diversity and richness of urban living. Her multilayered portfolio includes her work as a writer and published author, creativity coaching, and facilitation of leadership and well-being courses and workshops. She speaks at conferences and events, adding her voice to what feeds and nourishes our souls and spirits. A nature and tree lover, she brings the world of nature into her work at every opportunity and sees that as the voice of her creative spirit at work. She is the curator and host of the online Paper Therapy course and is currently hard at work on her fifth book.

Website: www.jackeeholder.com
Email: info@jackeeholder.com
Twitter: @jackeeholder

Orange Disks and Orange Balls 36

How a Visual Storyteller Stopped Self-Sabotaging

Francesca Aniballi

When I first spoke to Julia, she said she was always finding ways of hijacking her creative projects and that she felt all over the place. Julia was a visual storyteller, doing storyboarding and writing her own stories. She explained to me that her work had "two souls": on the one hand, she was a reflective blogger and a "social worker–storyteller" dealing with issues such as cooperation, acceptance, and discrimination against women and minority groups; on the other hand, she worked on her beloved visual stories about spiritual concepts and new ways of seeing the world.

Julia always felt "calm excitement" when she got lost in the creative process, but for some time, she had been feeling frustrated and easily irritable lately, especially when people and circumstances came in the way of her genuine self-expression. In our first coaching session, I asked her to describe a specific situation when she had felt triggered. She said a bad traffic jam had sent her mind reeling.

She said: "There were too many obstacles in my way."

I asked her if she was willing to play a bit. She nodded.

"Okay, then—take the first object you have in front of you," I said.

She picked up a small glass jar full of little colorful disks. She opened the jar and selected some orange disks. I asked her to write down her previous statement, replacing the word "obstacles" with what came to mind. She wrote: "There are a lot of oranges in my way."

Then I asked her to select a second object on her desk. She picked a small clown doll. I had her speak out her last statement in the clown's voice.

Julia burst into laughing as she spoke in a funny voice about all the oranges in her way.

From there, we imagined what else her clown persona could do with the oranges.

She said: "I am juggling with oranges . . . they are turning into orange balls."

Julia imagined playing with soft orange balls.

After 10 minutes of playful imaginative activity, she felt considerably lighter and amused. We went on to explore the ways that she sabotaged her creative projects. It turned out it was difficult for Julia to focus and to start her 'creative engine' when she felt stressed, anxious, or irritated. Besides, she always had too many ideas at once.

I asked Julia to write a short statement about the concept of 'focus.'

She wrote: "Focus is something other people do, and I can do it, too."

After a few seconds, she added that her statement did not feel real to her.

I asked her to close her eyes, breathe slowly, and retrieve the first memory she had revolving around 'focus.'

She told me about sitting for her Higher exam, trying to progress to the next level in her reading comprehension skills but being unable to do so. In every exam, her paper would always be the same color (i.e., level), and she could never progress to the next because she felt stuck. Her thoughts would race, and she would freeze into immobility, with tears in her eyes.

I guided Julia through a short writing assignment in which she had to fill in the blanks:

Higher colors are _____ when _____ and fly out of_____. Then _____, I can _____, and finally _____

She wrote the following: "Higher colors are fun when I play and fly out of hand. Then I smile, I can feel, and finally I am happy."

I drew Julia's attention to her use of the word "feel" and asked her where she could feel 'focused attention' in her body. She pointed to her upper chest, saying that she often felt heavy and stuck there, when she was overwhelmed by a brand-new project about to be started.

Her 'head' was full of ideas and excitement for the unknown, but she felt stuck in her chest. In the time we had remaining, I helped Julia focus her locus of awareness from her head to her chest, to listen to her bodily sensations and acknowledge them.

I also offered her the tool of 15-minute-break rewards. To feel empowered, she would have to take back her agency. I asked Julia to jot down in advance the small rewards she could give herself during the first stage of a creative project, in line with the way she was feeling on a specific day. Thus, after 15 minutes of work, she would have a break and give herself a small reward: a cup of chocolate, a favorite song, a poem to read, and so on. This would help her to move away from self-criticism and blame, into a space of self-nurture, until her creative project flowed with ease.

Over the following weeks, both on Zoom and by email, she reported her progress, which was small at first but gradually more significant.

We also worked on her perception of success and what that meant to her. I asked her to think of two people who were successful in her eyes. She mentioned her therapist and her hairdresser. I asked how they went after what they wanted. Julia said they didn't create any obstacles, had "the right mindset," and had supportive husbands. They owned their own business or practice.

I suggested that Julia should interview herself, and together we drafted the following questions:

1. What made you decide to branch out on your own on your creative path? What was the no-turning-back point?
2. Do you regret it?
3. What did you enjoy most, and are you happy with the way it turned out? What would you change now?

Afterward, I instructed her to ask the same questions to her therapist and hairdresser. She did so, and reviewed both their answers and her own answers. She reported having more clarity and feeling more centered and validated in her own choices.

In her last email, she said she was turning "from sabotage to 'supertage,'" meaning "a way of making myself bigger and putting myself out there."

Julia realized that she had had a skewed perspective with regard to her own abilities, which had kept her procrastinating a good deal. We worked on focus together. Julia devised ways of uncluttering her workspace and her desk. She also started working on "highly portable" creative projects, which only required her to have her laptop, pens, and paper handy. Thus, she discovered the power of decluttering and the power of taking action in order to gain clarity and momentum. She said: "There is power in doing."

By stopping being caught up in chaos, drama, and disorganization and by no longer being triggered by other people's opinions, actions, and moods, Julia could move forward and into increased power.

She said that whenever she thought of those 'obstacles' as soft orange balls, she would smile and feel empowered. More important, Julia was able to connect the dots between self-awareness, self-observation, and the ability to focus. Regarding focus, she wrote me the following:

"I can see where I'm at now, what I can realistically put my time and attention towards, what I want to do and feel like doing in the moment." She felt "a quiet, introspective, aligned energy" as she realized that "having to think about and organize too many different thoughts, ideas, and projects takes a lot of space and energy."

Learning Points

1. Turn your negative perceptions around through the power of imaginative play. Replace a negative statement with a positive one.
2. Feel and acknowledge your bodily sensations because they point you towards the "real" issue. Usually, in the same spot, you will also find the "cure."
3. To gain clarity, learn from yourself and from others through the interview technique. Devise your own questions in line with the topic you are seeking clarity about.

Self-Coaching Questions

1. How do you procrastinate or sabotage your creative projects? Make a list of all the ways you do so and tick them off every time you catch yourself. Make sure to replace them with positive action!
2. Where do you feel the sensation of being stuck in your body? Write down a dialogue with that body part to find out more.
3. How can you increase your self-awareness? Can you schedule a few minutes of quiet introspection every day?

About Francesca Aniballi

Francesca Aniballi, PhD, is a certified Artbundance Coach and art counselor who works with would-be or stuck creatives and people from all walks of life who want to express themselves more. She believes that creativity can empower, inspire, and uplift. She works with a number of creative techniques and processes to facilitate personal, creative, and spiritual unfoldment in her clients. She writes a blog under the pen name Frances Fay. You can find out about her at www.francesfay.it or email her at francesca.aniballi@gmail.com.

Bumping Into Walls   **37**

Navigating the Maze of Creativity

Lori Barraco Sylvester

JD sent me a text a few days ago. "Today I sent my first story collection to a freelance editor I hired." "That's great," I replied. "Congratulations!" I reflected on this good news and the process we shared that allowed him to reach this significant milestone toward his creative goal: self-publishing his collection of short stories before retirement.

During the initial conversation that preceded our 12 creativity coaching sessions, JD said, "I feel like I'm in a maze; what I want is at the other side, and I know I will bump into lots of walls finding the path through."

JD was educated, middle class, and a few years away from retirement, but his formal training was in software development, a field unrelated to creative writing and literature. He had taken college classes and participated in numerous writing critique groups as he developed his stories. However, when it came to publishing, JD felt overwhelmed, and this led to inertia. He decided, with some reservation, to try creativity coaching.

During our first meeting, he warned me: "I'm a tough person to coach. I don't like to feel manipulated or coerced into accepting cookie-cutter solutions that don't address my particular issues."

His concern is a challenge for all creativity coaches: tailoring the skills and strategies we've learned towards each unique client. I chose the "Self-Assessment Checklist for Writers" from Eric Maisel's *Become a Creativity Coach Now* to give me—and my client—a clearer picture of JD's strengths and weaknesses.

We met at quiet restaurants for our coaching sessions. It was JD's idea. He often wrote in such places; the setting felt creatively stimulating to him. "I have nine stories almost ready to publish, but it seems that the more I learn about fiction writing, the more I see the flaws in my work. I feel inadequate and wonder why I should bother."

JD had bumped into his first wall: lack of confidence. He didn't know where to start. I wanted to do two things right away: give him a task that didn't require an overwhelming amount of creative energy and put him in physical proximity to his writing by getting it off the computer and into his hands. I suggested he print the stories he wanted to publish and assemble the draft copies in a binder. It was a small step, one he agreed he could take. I also gave him a copy of the checklist to complete and bring to our next session.

When we met next, JD recounted his experience with the binder. "Once I put the stories in a binder, it felt like I had an actual book in my hand. I started arranging the stories in an order that made sense. I added a table of contents and found a great quote that summed up the theme of the collection. I can start to see this working." We were back on the path through the maze.

Then I asked about the writer's checklist. It was complete, and I looked it over. First, I looked for strengths. JD has confidence in his talent and skill as a writer. I also looked for mental health issues. When JD signed the coaching agreement before our first session, I made it clear that coaching is not therapy and that those concerns need to be addressed with a mental health professional. He said he had that covered. When I looked at the items he had marked, it confirmed that the creative paralysis he felt was linked to the exhaustion of engaging with the writing marketplace.

"I don't seem able to write anything new. All I can think about are these stories I haven't been able to revise. I write software for a living; it requires its own level of creativity. I tell myself that when I get home, I don't have the energy to plough back into doing more of the same activity. But now I realize that it's thinking about all the effort publishing requires that makes me so tired."

The next wall loomed before us: lack of energy. "Select one story from your binder that you want to revise," I suggested. "Tell yourself you're going to work on a page or two." My goal was to create a workload that would reduce the sense of exhaustion from facing an overwhelming task.

At our next session, JD reported some progress. "I decided to start with a story I wrote about baseball. There are still issues, but I made a few changes that make the story more cohesive and powerful, particularly around the ending." He had told me once that endings were hard for him to write.

As he finished talking, he took a deep breath and audibly sighed. The sigh alerted me to something else, something unsaid. "That's great news, "I replied, "but it seems that you're still hesitant around the revision process."

He thought about this. "I just don't understand how an author creates an excellent piece of work."

Our new wall: lack of experience.

JD was struggling, like many people who embark on their passion later in life, with the lack of a skill set that students and professionals typically acquire when they are young. "Try this," I offered. "Read what you consider to be a great short story. Then critique it; figure out what makes the story work."

He perked up at this suggestion. "I do enjoy reading. Critiquing someone else's story feels like less pressure than facing my own stuff."

"So, here's what's going on," JD announced at our next session. "When I sit down, ready to revise a story, I realize that I wrote it several years ago, and I'm not that person anymore. I'm finding that my narrative voice now won't match what's on the page."

He also told me he had joined a literary reading group to become a better writer but now spends so much time studying complex novels that he doesn't have time to write. "I feel like my tank is empty" was how he phrased it. I saw that he was re-engaged with the writing process, but his energy was scattered. We identified this new wall: lack of direction. After some discussion, he understood that he wouldn't be able to address his problem with consistent narrative voice unless he made time to write. He decided to limit his time with the book group and give himself permission to skip a book that he wasn't interested in, freeing up time to spend revising his work.

When we met again, JD clearly had found new energy for his writing. "All that great literature I'd been reading finally paid off. I'm a more critical reader when it comes to my own stories. I can make these quick connections, like lights flashing." But with this new energy came a new challenge, another wall: he had lost an earlier version of a story he wanted to revise; he wanted to see how the story looked in that earlier form and to start the revision process from that point.

But instead of getting stuck, he got himself back on the path. "I imagined I was an engineer repairing a bridge. I need to keep the whole thing stabilized while removing and replacing parts without the whole structure collapsing." He saw how his skills developing software enhanced rather than impeded his personal writing experience. "That's actually how large software projects are revised and upgraded. You modify small pieces and let the changes ripple through."

It was obvious that JD's confidence in his ability to revise his stories and maneuver around the walls of his maze had improved dramatically. I decided to take a proactive step. "When we first met, you said that being stuck on the revision process got in the way of developing new work. What about writing something new?" I could see when he lowered his eyes, a wall loomed up: fear of failure.

"I wrote a paragraph several years ago while on vacation, something that felt like the start of a story, but I never went back to it." The only way back on the path was to revisit that paragraph and try to expand it in some way. We scheduled our next session in two months to give him time to get something written down.

"I wrote the draft of that story," he said when we met again. "It was like the maze we've been navigating. When I got stuck, I knew that it was just a wall. The path was there; I just had to keep looking. Now I have 10 stories." He had also decided to divide his collection into two books. Publishing five stories seemed more manageable than all 10 at once.

JD had reached the point where he needed time to settle into this new process of revising, writing, and reading. Outside the restaurant, we shook hands. "Thank you for all your help," he said. "How about I get in touch with you if I wander down another dead end?"

I knew there would be other dead ends, other walls blocking JD's progress, but he was now fully engaged in the process of creative writing, and he would see those walls as nothing more than part of that process. "Sounds good," I said, "but let me know how you're doing, even if you don't get stuck."

Learning Points

1. When you feel overwhelmed by a task that seems insurmountable, break it into manageable parts. The success you experience when you accomplish a task can produce the energy you need to keep moving forward.
2. Appreciate the walls for what they are, an indicator of where the true path lies. There are a finite number of walls to bump into. Each time you overcome an obstacle, you eliminate another false path.
3. Remember to see the wall or obstacle for what it is, not what you imagine it to be.

Self-Coaching Questions

1. Are there issues in your life that are not related to your artistic discipline that interfere with your ability to be creative?

2. Do you recognize and acknowledge milestones? These are the signs that let you know you are making progress.
3. Are you investing time and energy in the skill set required by your chosen craft?

About Lori Barraco Sylvester

Lori practices creativity coaching in the Albany, New York, area. As a visual artist who has faced and overcome her own walls over the years, she has developed an interest in helping people find their way along their own creative paths. She has a particular interest in working with clients who are nearing retirement and want to begin or reconnect with a long-held creative dream. You can contact Lori through her website at www.creativetransitions. vpweb.com.

The Cracks in the Pavement

38

Liminal Spaces and Creativity

Litza Bixler

"What is your first memory of being creative?"

I often ask this question to reveal clients' creative stories, to get a sense of their beliefs about creativity and how these beliefs might be affecting their current situation.

Susanne pauses and stares upward, searching. "I guess in a way, it was dancing as a little girl, but because I connect that so much to my work. . . ." She trails off.

Susanne came to me at a threshold in her career. She'd already made several significant transitions in her life: she'd been a professional dancer, a massage therapist, and a choreographer with her own company. Then she became a mother and moved to the countryside. Most recently, she returned to the city with her family and began a freelance choreographer career. Now, she was at a crossroads once again, attempting to determine her best path forward.

In session, she continues exploring the meaning of the word 'creative.'

". . . It also stimulates other memories, like when I was at junior school, and I was just making stuff . . . those other creative activities were more playful. Dance didn't have as much space around it; it almost feels like it's owned by . . . I don't know, maybe people saw that I had some talent, so they wanted to nurture it, and they jumped on it." Susanne pauses and looks down. I remain silent. I want her to have the space to continue.

". . . My mum, deep down, she wanted to be dancer and didn't have the opportunity, so there was a lot of her own journey in that; then dance quite quickly gets driven into something, and it's already a career when I'm 13! But whenever I make stuff with the kids, it feels like nobody even cares, nobody's bothered about it. I just really enjoy making stuff."

Guiding creative play into a career at a relatively young age is a common story in the performing arts. Training begins very young and often requires parental support. So, an activity that was once fun and enjoyable gradually morphs into something that is governed by market forces and the expectations of others. Consequently, even as an adult, it can be difficult for creative people to separate their dreams from those of their childhood caregivers.

Similarly, when the word 'work' is attached to creativity, it can sometimes suck the joy out of it. The motivation to create can become extrinsic rather than intrinsic, burdening the creative act with financial obligations, deadlines and pressure. When this happens, creativity is no longer about play and process but about product and productivity.

Susanne touches on this when I ask her about detaching creativity from 'work.'

She says, "I guess if I'm not doing it for work, I don't really know where creativity sits." She pauses and stares into the middle distance.

I ask Susanne whether she thinks she can carve out some time for creative play. "Yes," she says, "I've been doodling and drawing a bit lately already."

"And what's the smallest amount of time that you could commit to this?" I ask. She says 15 minutes a day feels achievable. I then ask what a space for creative play might look like for her.

"I suppose it's like somewhere I can try things and express things, where I'm not within the confines of our society or doing what I'm supposed to be doing. You know, I was just saying the other day, it's like . . . being in between the cracks of the pavement. When I play, I sort of weave in between things. That's what creativity feels like for me."

There's often a moment in a session when I feel the significance of a turn of phrase, a memory, or a story. I feel the energy shift and intensify. I get a tingling sensation, an electric pulse that signals to me, here, listen; this is something. Whether this happens at the beginning of the session or later on, it often gets to the heart of things and illuminates the session's core theme.

"That's an interesting choice of words," I say. I ask her whether she's familiar with the idea of liminal spaces. When she says she isn't, I explain that a liminal space is the space in between, a sort of limbo. The concept of liminality was developed by anthropologist Victor Turner as a means of describing the middle stage of a rite of passage. The word comes from *limen*, meaning 'threshold.'

This idea of symbolic thresholds occurs in many different cultures. For example, the Aboriginal Australian experience of 'going walkabout' creates a liminal space out in the wild. Adolescents undertake this journey to prove that they are capable of survival, but the journey is also a rite of passage. The child is essentially walking through adolescence to arrive at a new adult identity. Similarly, when a husband carries his wife over the threshold of the home, it symbolizes the transition from single to married. Pregnancy is also a liminal space between *not motherhood* and *motherhood*. And it is common for creative people to talk about being pregnant with ideas or to refer to their projects as babies. Also, in many stories and folktales, doorways, windows, portals, wormholes, wells, rabbit holes, and caves are also thresholds. They are literal links between worlds, physical spaces that the hero must pass through in order to arrive at a new symbolic life.

I often use doorways, with their imaginary locks, keys, and 'open me' spells, as spaces where potential can bloom. Because when the client is faced with a door, he or she can imagine any number of new worlds on the other side.

I ask Susanne to actually stand in a doorway of her choosing. Then I ask her to note that she is no longer in one room or another, that she is now literally and figuratively *in between*. A house is a useful metaphor because people move back and forth through rooms. When a person leaves a room, it doesn't disappear. The room is still an accessible space. Also, people can walk through one room to get to another, just as they can walk through their current life in order to arrive at a new one.

Once she is standing 'on the threshold,' I ask her to visualize the room she has just left as her current life. Then, she imagines several new rooms, each of which represents a potential life-path. One room is a new and improved version of her current life. Another represents "training as a dance therapist." A third symbolizes "opening an art center."

I ask her to focus on each of these spaces. What do they look like, feel like, sound like? Is the air cool or warm or hot? Does the space feel small or large? Once she has these potential spaces clear in her mind, I ask to drop into her body and sense whether she feels a physical pull toward any of the rooms, including the previous one.

Susanne reports that she felt a "gentle tug" toward the "creating an art center" room.

She says, "The other rooms were fine, but much smaller and narrower and not as multifaceted," whereas "the art center room felt like it was incorporating my current life as well. I felt like I had more space to expand my body in there. Just being in the movement therapy room felt a bit heady."

When we return to these ideas in a later session, Susanne shares that during the previous week she discovered a huge sense of freedom in the 'in between' and that it seemed to open her mind to multiple possibilities.

She notes that she found herself "thinking more about what I wanted to do in the future. I realized that I've been so busy chasing my tail, I haven't really thought about the bigger picture."

"So, this focus on the bigger picture, is that the intention now?" I ask.

"Yes" she says, "I think so."

Instead of setting aside a specific 15-minute window for creative play, Susanne says she found herself "doodling in the gaps, for example, finding tiny moments during busy rehearsals to play." This was a variation on what we initially planned, but it seemed to serve the same function.

For now, Susanne decides that she wants to remain on the threshold. For her, liminality encourages expansive 'blue-sky thinking,' and it keeps her focused on the bigger picture. After she has explored her options, she can then choose to step over the threshold and into a new life.

I finish the session with a meditation that asks Susanne to visualize herself in the cracks in the pavement; to imagine herself in the gaps in between muscle and bone, skin and air, earth and universe. I ask her to feel her body rise up into the air and to notice that there is a moment when she could be flying or falling or floating. Then I ask her if it's possible to hold multiple pathways in her mind, and to consider that she could follow these paths simultaneously. I want her to suspend the pressure of 'this or that,' 'either/or,' 'forward or backward'—because it is here, in the gaps in between, that her creative potential can flourish.

Learning Points

1. It's important to allow creativity to be about play and process; to detach it from the idea of 'work.' External motivators can be useful, but before we worked, we were children who were intrinsically motivated to create. Play is how we learn in a low-stakes environment, so it's an important part of the creative process.
2. Liminal spaces are full of creative potential, so choosing to remain on the threshold can be a powerful choice.
3. Liminality can also lead to anxiety, especially in a world that prizes decisiveness and action. So, the creative person should seek out support during this time and accept that being on the threshold can generate some uncomfortable feelings.

Self-Coaching Questions

1. What would it be like to remain on the threshold? Can you remember other times in your life when you found yourself on a threshold?
2. What would it feel like to create from delight? What would it feel like to enjoy the creative process without caring about the final product?
3. What would it be like to hold multiple potential paths in your mind? What would it be like to follow these paths simultaneously?

About Litza Bixler

Litza Bixler is a creative polymath with a wealth of experience across a wide range of art forms, including film, fine art, choreography, and writing. She is a certified Kaizen-Muse Creativity Coach, with additional certificates in counseling and hypnotherapy. She also has a master's in dance anthropology with additional training in a broad range of dance and somatic techniques. Litza set up Compasso Coaching to help others discover their own *true north* and navigate their journey with compassion, creativity and courage. Whether your intention is to build a successful creative business, to generate new creative habits, to boost your creative practice, or to bring more creativity into your parenting, your relationships, or your daily life; Compasso Coaching can help you find your way. Visit www.compassocoaching.com and www.litzabixler.com.

A Leadership Journey to Purpose   **39**

Personal Breakthroughs From Leading Others

Tania Kelvin

I was stuck. I wasn't creating. I was coaching others to get in touch with their own creativity and unique voice of personal expression, yet I had barely scratched the surface of my own unique gifts as an artist. I was not fully free myself yet or doing what I've dreamt of with my talents. I have big dreams, to the point of their feeling scary and seeming unachievable.

Even though creativity comes in many forms and I did apply it in other ways in the past decade, including marketing, photography, digital arts (graphics, images, video, audio), home decorating, and day-to-day problem solving, I was stalling, stiff, and buried in my negative emotions about doing what I really wanted. It sounds crazy, but felt real . . . that the thing I wanted to do and that I enjoyed doing scared me to do. By having the chance years before to try various art forms and mediums in art school, I realized that I loved to create with my hands, whether that would be sculpting, painting, drawing, designing and fabricating jewelry, or dabbling in other mediums.

My perfectionism and judgments kicked in and I told myself things like, "I'm rusty. What if I can't live up to what I've done before? It's going to take a long time to learn. I'm older now and will take a very long time. I don't know how to do X, Y, and Z. I don't have what I need. I don't know how to do this as a business. I won't stay on track. I don't know the right people. I don't want to do X, Y, and Z. I'm not good enough." Those are just a sample, and there were more not relating to the art I enjoyed and dreamt of doing profession-ally. Many such thoughts crossed over into other areas of my life as well.

I was listening to my inner critic and ego, hearing negative beliefs from my own personal history. These were reruns of what others would tell me about leading a creative artist's life and what that means and entails, even if they didn't have personal experience and only came from what they heard and assumed. It all paralyzed my inner artist. I was in a straitjacket of my own making, listening to my downward spiraling thoughts, others' opinions, and fears and doubts. My passion, motivation, and drive were buried. The playful, colorful, carefree innocence of my inner artist as a child had been taken away from me. I was stuck and not creating works of beautiful art that were buried inside of me, dying to come out.

So, after doing a lot of self-care, personal development, and reflecting on life and myself, I took a leap out of my comfort zone and founded a Meetup group in my city to bring like-minded, creativity-loving people together and build my local tribe. I wanted to find great people to do fun things with around town involving culture and the arts, plus create offerings of workshops. I wanted the group's purpose to be to inspire, encourage, and explore creativity.

As a main offering, I started an in-person workshop for a small group to go deep through personal development with our creativity as the central focus, which, after all, affects all areas of life. For the 13-week group-coaching workshop, I used *The Artist's Way* by Julia Cameron as a textbook along with my teachings, coaching, and guidance. I trusted that the right people would be brought together and threw the idea out there and created this offering. The truth is, I needed it for myself also, as a leader, coach, and artist.

The five of us in the group ranged in age from our 30s to our early 70s and included both genders. Only one identified as a professional artist. Others either didn't consider themselves artistic or only somewhat creative in other areas of their lives or hobbyists on occasion or had done an art form before but hadn't touched it for years.

We met weekly. In the safe space that I created at one of their homes, the group bonded over the weeks, with a beautiful synergy of support from all. As a leader, I showed vulnerability through my own sharing, as I was also participating in all the exercises for my own journey and experiencing it alongside them, as we were in it together. I opened up about my struggles with doing my fine art, a passion of mine that I'd put away for so many years, years when I needed it the most.

Each week in the group, we all opened up more and more, and I realized that by coaching them, I was also coaching myself. Everything I said applied to me as well. As the leader, I had the most accountability. I needed to lead myself as a coach and be an example for the others. If I hadn't been the leader, I might not have been as active as I was. The workshop was a growth experience, and we made sure to celebrate our wins, no matter how large or small;

we laughed, we cried, we danced, we ate, and we took fun pictures of the group.

For the 13 weeks, I meditated often, worked on doing daily stream of consciousness writing what Julia Cameron calls "morning pages," reviewed affirmations, created new affirmations, heightened my awareness in all areas of my life through the exercises, focused on emotional intelligence, had solo fun activities weekly for my inner artist child, and signed up for an improv class (after not having done any performing arts for over a decade). I created other short workshops for my Meetup group, restarted to paint, realized how to view a mountain a step at a time, and created a new power statement as a way to see myself the way I wanted to be.

By being the giver and teaching others tools to implement for themselves, it brought a fresh new perspective to the teachings I had possessed before. It was evident that the workshop functioned at a deep level, emotionally, mentally, spiritually, and physically and involved a process that could not be rushed. For all of us, we gently planted a seed in our souls, had to nourish it, and had to give it love, attention, and a lot of patience for it to grow and flourish. There was a lot happening beneath the surface, so patience and keeping on with the process, especially through writing and paying attention to our thoughts, were keys.

The biggest breakthroughs for me came in my growth as a leader, seeing strengths I hadn't noticed or used before as I trusted my intuition to guide me in my teachings and coaching. The questions and observations for each individual that came out of my mouth sometimes made me think, "Wow, that was good!," which got me a good laugh. When I felt anxious, unprepared, stressed or fearful, I would take deep breaths and meditate. With ongoing mindset shifts in the direction of positive thoughts, I knew that all would be fine. I was able to turn the fear energy I felt in my body into the excitement of passion by thinking about why I was doing what I was doing, what I appreciated, the loving energy I was receiving from those in the group, and how much they trusted me.

There were many breakthroughs, both small and large. Participants began to say things like, "I can actually say now that I'm happy!," "I realize I actually am creative!," "I don't have to hide my art any longer," "I couldn't have done it without you and the group," and "I don't feel depressed." We celebrated each person's achievements and the little baby steps it took to get us there. I celebrated performing on stage in front of an audience for the first time in over a decade and creating my first painting in years, created in a new style and free of perfectionism. Most of all, I celebrated my biggest achievement, being the catalyst for each participant's transformations for a better life, including my own. It also felt amazing that I brought people together locally and we formed bonds and lifelong friendships by going through a group creativity coaching experience and by applying creativity to all areas of our lives.

Learning Points

1. Stepping out of your comfort zone in a leadership role is not only rewarding but is also an act of giving, both to yourself and others. Leadership comes with many benefits and creates many opportunities for growth.
2. Creating a safe space, being courageously vulnerable, and sharing personal experiences as a leader create a supportive environment for others to open up, communicate, release feelings, bond, and share on a deeper level.
3. Listen to your intuition about what your inner artist soul needs, give it loving attention, nourish it, allow it to express itself without judgments, patiently allow it to grow, and celebrate even small wins.

Self-Coaching Questions

1. What areas of your creative life do you lead in and could you lead in?
2. In what areas are you willing to take a stand for your personal growth and your creativity, including implementing changes by stepping out of your comfort zone?
3. What is one change you can make right now in support of your emotional, mental, spiritual, physical, and creative life?

About Tania Kelvin

Tania Kelvin is an artist who has made it her mission to coach others to creative breakthroughs. She decided to coach and empower others after emotional intelligence training and her own personal growth breakthroughs. Tania understands what it means to be creatively blocked and unfulfilled and her vision is to encourage inspiration, exploration, joy, and a life fully lived. You can find her at www.taniakelvin.com and follow her on social media platforms, @TaniaKelvin and @TaniaKelvinCreates.

The Magic of an Escape, a Goal, and a Deadline

A Playwright Finishes Her Musical and Writes a Play in a Week

Jenny Maguire

I had the good fortune of discovering Eric Maisel when I was working with a life coach of my own. I had recently moved to a new place that presented multilayered obstacles. Having a coach was a huge gift to me while navigating these turbulent waters.

One of my goals was to investigate the world of creativity coaching, something I had been doing instinctively with fellow artists for years without structure or financial reward. I googled "creativity coaching," and Eric Maisel was the main person to appear. To be honest, I was initially overwhelmed and intimidated by his impressive accomplishments. I took a deep breath, kept investigating, and to my surprise found his two-part online creativity coaching training program. Really? The person who created creativity coaching is that accessible and available to share his knowledge? What a gift. Not without some inner critic battles, I signed up. Eric's teachings and the inspiring weekly contributions of the artistic worldwide group were a game changer for me as an artist, a self-coach, and a coach for others.

From the very beginning, Eric encouraged us to learn by working with clients. He believes there is no better way to learn than by doing. I agreed and reached out to a couple of artist friends. I spoke with Hannah (not her real name) about what I was doing and asked if she would like to be one of my clients. Her response, "Of course. Anything for you, my love."

I know Hannah very well. We are dear friends, artistic collaborators, wearing many different creative hats on many projects over the years. I know she is a doer and would enter this relationship with an open heart and a game spirit. The key for me was setting up some structure around our communication so it wouldn't just be two gals who love and support each other chatting. Rather, I wanted her to experience me as a coach who supports, fosters, and encourages *her* creative goals. It wouldn't be about me, my problems or needs.

Hannah is a mother of three and a working actor. In her mid-30's, she went back to school, graduating valedictorian from her nursing program. Her passion for writing emerged when faced with a life-threatening medical condition. The day after major surgery, she picked up her computer and wrote a play she had always wanted to write. She said to herself, "It's now or never." That's Hannah: an artist, a doer, a survivor.

When we started coaching, Hannah was writing a new musical. Hannah and I discussed the many creative hats Hannah had worn over the years, gaining clarity on what was important to her now. What goals would be exciting yet could realistically be accomplishable in the next three months? Although Hannah had experienced self-initiated artistic success as a writer, she yearned for the validation and support of an artistic home. Hannah was clear that her "hyper-focus" (her primary goal) was to finish her musical and start the New Year with a reading. We also identified two supporting goals: find focused time to write and apply to a writer's residency program.

The major obstacles that Hannah identified during our initial sessions were the following two. First was, "I need more time to write." The second was the exhausting, fierce inner critics that scream, "What's the point? Am I ever going to find an artistic home? Am a masochist? Why keep writing if no one other than myself is going to produce my work?"

We started with the issue of time. We explored the idea of an early morning writing routine. I shared the top reasons why this is a good idea. She responded, "I totally agree. Just so hard to implement!" We exchanged alternative daily routine ideas: going to a place where she wouldn't be disturbed four times a week, attending a week-long writers' workshop, and getting childcare help during a particular part of the day. She said she was game to try. Yet I knew the demands on her time as a working mother would make it easier said than done.

Then she mentioned in one of our email exchanges that her in-laws were coming for a visit, and she dreamed of escaping for a few days when they were visiting. I had empathy for the obvious obstacles: the guilt, the expense, and the demands of three kids. Where would she go? And yet, I encouraged her instinct. I encouraged her to have a talk with her husband about her creative goals and how a writer's escape would help her accomplish them. As her coach, I felt confident that if she got a couple of days to do nothing but write, she would finish her musical or get pretty darn close. Once her *butt was in the chair*, she was a force of artistic nature.

I hadn't heard from Hannah in a week, so I texted "How are you?" and she responded, "Amazing! I am on my way to an inn that was the home to where a famous composer used to write his musicals." Hannah and her friend from high school, who is a painter, were on their way to have an artistic escape. Her friend was inspired by the work Hannah and I were doing and got her own creativity coach. I was thrilled by her unexpected and inspiring reply. The escape weekend was a big artistic win. Did Hannah finish that musical by the end of the year and have a reading in the New Year? You bet your *butt in chair* she did.

After a successful reading of her musical, Hannah became daunted by the task of finding a composer. Her inner critic began to raise its ugly head.

Part of our text coaching read:

Hannah: I feel like I have been putting my energies into entities with no return. Not just this . . . just feel like I need to reexamine. Am I just a masochist?

Me: It's normal to feel frustrated re: effort vs reward. Will send more on that. No not a masochist, just an individual & an artist, don't think you could exist without creating.

Hannah: Thank you love. Sorry to be a downer. How are you?

Me: Well, I mean you would exist of course without creating but me thinks you would feel pretty down, empty & get depressed. You are not a downer. A human being with feelings & needs & we get exhausted & need some validation. You are not a machine. Take a deep breath. Be kind to yourself. You are just coming off the highs of finishing your play, submitting & having a reading. It's a big deal. Did you feel good after the reading? This is the beginning of another creative challenge. Can you think of a realistic goal/s around finding a composer, maybe a 1–3-month goal? What is making it feel so hard? The work itself or the patience around the work?

Hannah: Thank you. I did feel good about the reading and the accomplishment . . . I made a deal with myself that I would work on finding a composer for 15–30 mins a day. The enormity of the reality of finding a composer is just paralyzing.

Me: I love the deal you made with yourself. Yes, the big picture is always overwhelming, it's why we have to break it down, like you are doing. Keep returning to our beginner's heart & letting go of expectations.

The text exchanged continued; we hashed out next step ideas. It ended with Hannah sending me a link to one of her dream composers. After many months of small actionable steps, her dream composer signed on.

I signed up for Dr. Eric Maisel's Advanced Creativity Coaching course, and Hannah and I continued to work together. At the end of one of our phone sessions, Hannah said, "I may be crazy, but I am thinking about applying for the playwriting Relentless Award, which comes with a cash prize. I need to find a way to pay for my composer and not have to sell one of my kids. The deadline is in two weeks, and I have this very personal play in my head that needs to come out."

If it was anyone else, I would have thought "Write and submit a play in two weeks? Yes, that is crazy and unrealistic." Yet I knew Hannah. I knew if we came up with a well-laid plan for *finding the time to write*, she could make the deadline and have a new play written. We both got really inspired. Embracing the meaning of relentless, she again got her *butt in the seat*.

For the next week, every day, she would go to her favorite *do not disturb* place and write fearlessly, without judgment. Just let it out.

I texted her daily, offering questions and thoughts taken from Dr. Eric Maisel's lessons:

- What is a creative practice? It is a way that you take your existence seriously, one breath at a time, one thought at a time.
- You are practicing the quiet heroics of the trinity: truth, beauty, and goodness.

And adding some of my own:

- Are you honoring your creative spirit at your sacred space?
- Is your relentless spirit in the driver's seat?

Two weeks later, I wrote this to the Advanced Creativity Coaching Group in response to a text from Hannah that read: "I just submitted. My Mother's Day gift to myself."

"My client wrote a play in a week! Giving me enough time to read predeadline and be absolutely blown away by it. It was so shockingly good I felt like I had to take a nap after I read it. It hit me in the gut & took me on an emotional roller coaster. For all the right reasons. And it was hilarious & poetic & some of her best writing. Since she wrote it in one week, we had enough time for me to read it, have a creative coaching notes jam session and have her tweak her artistic statement. Her submission is stellar & she did it with a two-week deadline! Relentless!"

In the first six months we worked together, Hannah accomplished her primary goal and her two supporting goals and embraced the unexpected creative challenges that arise when an artist makes meaning. We continue to coach and collaborate today.

Learning Points

1. Find your *audience of one.* Hannah said, "I couldn't have done all those things without your love and support and your crazy talent as a creativity coach." I recall a now well-known novelist and playwright telling the story of writing his first novel, being texted every day by a person who believed in him, who would ask, "Are you writing?" He said that it made all the difference.
2. Find the time. Find the escape. Get your *butt in the chair.* Don't be afraid to ask yourself and your family for what you need. Yes, the in-laws might be a little 'miffed,' but mama comes home refreshed, accomplished, happy, and empowered. I say that is a win for everyone.
3. Don't be afraid to jump off the crazy cliff, take a risk, and get obsessed. It was a great learning moment for me to see how powerful finding the right meaning opportunity, the right goal, and a deadline are for motivating a writer. Hannah never would've tackled this incredibly personal, major anxiety-producing material without the influence of this potential money grant and their call for raw, unfiltered, brave material. It freed her up to write without self-censorship and the fear of not doing it right. The outcome was delicious, satisfying, and therapeutic on so many levels.

Self-Coaching Questions

1. Who are your inner circle creative support system? Have you considered getting a creativity coach? How would it feel to have a totally supportive, nonjudgmental, personal artistic cheerleader who wants to know you and has nothing but your best creative interest at heart? What is that worth to you?
2. Look at your calendar. Is there a day or a weekend for an artistic escape? Would you go by yourself or call and inspire an artistic friend? Envision where you would go; do a little dream google research. What environment inspires you to get in the zone? What project could you dive into and accomplish more in two days than you manage to do in several weeks of everyday distractions?

3. What is your inspiration? Your goal? Your deadline? Are you seeking a grant? A commission? An award? What is going to motivate you to get an artistic idea out of your head and into the world?

About Jenny Maguire

Jenny is a mama, an actor, VO artist, filmmaker and producer, and creativity coach. As a very wise director said to her, "It's not about taking away; it's about adding on." An actor by trade, Jenny has also served as a producer, creator, and consultant on several film and theatre projects. Most recently, Jenny is one of the five female leads and consulting producer on the fiercely independent, female-driven film *STUCK*. After a brief stint on the West Coast, Jenny returned to her New York creative community, landing in beautiful Beacon, New York, where she is inspired daily by the kind, diverse, artistic community. Jenny embraces her yin for the development of new works and helping others and her yang for performing and making things happen. Intrigued? Go to jennymaguirecreative.com (creativity coaching) and jennymaguireactor.com (actor).

Appendix

Tips for Creativity Coaches and Prospective Coaches

What Is Coaching?

Coaching is simply helping another person. You draw on your life experience and your wisdom, and you learn by doing. There is no other way to learn but by doing. That means that your first clients are getting an unseasoned you—but someone has to get an unseasoned you! Most coaching programs use the dyadic peer model: two coaches-in-training coaching each other. You can learn by coaching a peer, by coaching a buddy, by coaching volunteer clients, and so on, but you will only learn by actually coaching.

What else do you need, in addition to doing? Well, you probably need some basic principles and guidelines, about being of help, about being respectful, about working from a client-centered perspective, about providing support, about holding clients accountable, and so on. You need to think about what's transpired after it's transpired. You need courage, a helping attitude, compassion, and your wits about you. Those are the tasks of a coach and the skill set of a coach.

What is the work? The work is both helping clients with the issues they raise and also identifying issues they have not raised. How do you help? You ask clarifying questions that cause a client to think. You wonder aloud about whether a client might want to try X, Y, or Z. You offer suggestions. You propose exercises. You teach—maybe a cognitive technique, a breathing technique, or an organizational technique. You are 'in it' with your client, using whatever you have in your human arsenal to help your client deal with her challenges and solve her problems. You are being of help. That is the work.

Coaching is helping a person with the thing he says he wants changed or improved. Maybe he can't say what it is he wants improved; then you help identify what's wanted. One tennis player may want to be coached on his backhand; another may "want to get better" and is hoping that you can spot where he can improve. That is, a client may come in with concrete issues ("If I could manage to write and sell my novel, my life would feel much more meaningful!") or with a global, amorphous need ("I don't know what I need, but I know that I've had problems with meaning since childhood").

With one client, you so-to-speak work on his backhand, and with another client, you work on every part of his game. That is, with a client who feels that his main concern is getting recognized as a writer, you help him do exactly what he says he wants to do: write his novel, sell it, have a career, make his mark, and so on. You take him at his word and focus where he asks you to focus. With another client, you work on every part of his game, either because he has expressed that many things aren't working (his backhand, his forehand, his serve, his court movement, and so on) or because he can't name what exactly isn't working.

What is the actual work? Well, if a client says, "I think that if I felt more confident, stopped letting my mate walk all over me, finally gave my dad a piece of my mind, and got my painting career started, I would feel a lot better," you help her plan how she is going to feel more confident, stop letting her mate walk all over her, give her dad a piece of her mind, and get her painting career started. Your client has done a lovely job of explaining to you where she wants help; then you start to help.

Over time, you hone your skills. These include your listening skills, your ability to empathize, your ways of being direct, your ways of holding another person accountable, and so on. There are many helping skills to hone over time, from problem-solving skills to skills of personal presence. These skills fall into two rough categories: skills that help you support your client and skills that help you hold a client accountable. You are both a cheerleader and a taskmaster, and both skill sets require honing.

You deal with everything and anything except for those things that you can't or shouldn't deal with. You deal in a common-sense way with all sorts of psychological matters but you don't "diagnose and treat mental disorders," whatever that phrase means. That is really the chief difference between coaching and psychotherapy. Coaches need to be psychological, but we don't "diagnose and treat mental disorders." You also don't offer legal advice, medical advice, and so on. But you do offer lots of advice and suggestions in many, many areas.

What Does Coaching Look Like?

What is it that a coach actually does? Well, whether you're doing creativity coaching, life coaching, spiritual coaching, business coaching, or some other coaching, you will probably learn to do all of the following 24 things—let's call them tactics. These 24 tactics constitute the nuts and bolts of coaching. Let me run through them using two examples, one a writer named Jack and one a writer named Mary.

1. You offer an opening.

This sounds like:

"Hi, Jack, very nice to be working with you. What's on your mind?"

Or:

"Hi, Mary, very nice to be working with you. You mentioned a lot of issues in your email to me—where do you think you'd like to start?"

2. You ask clarifying questions.

This sounds like:

"Jack, you mentioned that you started three novels before starting this one. What happened with those?"

Or:

"Mary, you mentioned in your email that you hadn't completed any of your previous novels. Can you tell me a little bit more about that?"

3. You interrupt to clarify.

This sounds like:

"Jack, I didn't quite get that. Can you explain that a little bit more?"

Or:

"Mary, you say that you have a quiet room with a desk but I think you just said that you prefer to write in the living room with a lot of noise all around you. Can you clarify that a little for me?"

4. You interrupt for emphasis.

This sounds like:

"Jack, what you just said strikes me as important! Can we stay there for a minute?"

Or:

"Mary, I wonder if that rude rejection letter is what caused you to stop writing. Can we look at that a little bit more?"

5. You make suggestions.

This sounds like:

"Jack, I have a suggestion. The novel of yours that you were just talking about, it sounds so near to completion, I wonder if it's time to maybe complete it. What do you think?"

Or:

"Mary, you know, you might try writing in a café if your husband and your kids bother you too much at home. What are your thoughts about that?"

6. You identify potential problems.

This sounds like:

"Jack, you say that you want to start a morning writing practice, but you also say that you like to stay out late. Do you think that the staying out late might get in the way of your ability to get up early and write?"

Or:

"Mary, you say that your in-laws will be visiting and that you have to entertain them a lot. Will that get in the way of your writing schedule?"

7. You clarify goals.

This sounds like:

"Okay, Jack, it sounds like you'd like to complete that older novel before really launching the new one. Is that the goal, then, finishing that older novel?"

Or:

"Okay, Mary, it sounds like the goal is to be able to write regularly in the context of your busy, demanding life. Is that a fair way to state the goal?"

8. You plan and schedule.

This sounds like:

"Okay, Jack, how many days during the coming week do you want to work on your novel, and how many hours a day do you want to devote to it?"

Or:

"Okay, Mary, let's create a schedule that helps you keep writing while your in-laws are visiting."

9. You teach.

This sounds like:

"Jack, you know, there are a lot of reasons why writers have trouble finishing their books. Let me share a few of those reasons with you and see if any of them ring a bell."

Or:

"Mary, let me share with you why I think it would be great if you could institute a morning writing practice. I think there are three important reasons for giving that a try."

10. You create a sense of solidarity.

This sounds like:

"Okay, Jack, let's see how we're going to tackle this next challenge!"

Or:

"Okay, Mary, let's put our heads together and see what we can come up with!"

11. You cheerlead, encourage, and support.

This sounds like:

"Wow, Jack, getting 5,000 words done this week is great. Congrats on that!"

Or:

"Wow, Mary, actually managing to write while your in-laws were around is amazing. Congrats on that!"

12. You invite accountability.

This sounds like:

"Okay, Jack, I want to suggest the following. If you're willing, I'd like to have you check in weekly via email on your goals. What do you think about that?"

Or:

"Mary, what are your thoughts on a short daily email check-in? You'd just let me know that you'd got to your writing or, if you hadn't, that you intended to get to it tomorrow. What do you think about that?"

13. You repeat and confirm.

This sounds like:

"Okay, Jack, let me see if I've got this right. You want to get a thousand words done each day as you work to complete your novel. Is that right?"

Or:

"Okay, Mary, let me just double check to see if I have this right. You want to try to write six days a week and then get in some painting on Sundays. Is that right?"

14. You check in on goals.

This sounds like:

"Okay, Jack, last week you set the goal of writing six days out of seven. How did that go?"

Or:

"Okay, Mary, you hoped to write for an hour a day despite having your in-laws visiting. How did that go?"

15. You reframe and offer alternatives.

This sounds like:

"Jack, absolutely, you could look at self-publishing as a complete negative. But I'd like to point out a few positives to self-publishing."

Or:

"Mary, I know you're holding your in-laws visit as a catastrophe, but I wonder if there's a way we can look at it as an opportunity for you to learn how to write 'in the middle of things'?"

16. You focus on cognitions.

This sounds like:

"Jack, I think I heard you just say that you're no good at public speaking and don't want to do book signings when your book comes out. I wonder if that's a thought that serves you very much?"

Or:

"Mary, you just said that you find it impossible to write unless you check your emails first. I wonder if that 'impossible' is really an 'impossible' or maybe something else?"

17. You focus on behaviors.

This sounds like:

"Jack, you say that you have to read the newspaper and check online news before you get to your writing each day. Can you tell about how long you spend on that?"

Or:

"So, Mary, you say that when you get an idea you're not in the habit of writing it right down. I wonder if we can change that behavior and get you in the habit of writing down your ideas when they come to you."

18. You ask for updates.

This sounds like:

"Jack, you know, I haven't checked in recently about those blog posts you were hoping to get written. Want to catch me up on how that went?"

Or:

"Mary, we were also going to keep track of whether you were getting to your Sunday painting, but I haven't asked about that for a while. How has that been going?"

19. You send your client out to investigate.

This sounds like:

"Okay, Jack, since going to a writer's conference interests you, why don't you look into writers' conferences and report back on what you find out?"

Or:

"Okay, Mary, we're getting very close to having you submit to literary agents. Want to investigate the world of agents and come up with a list of agents you intend to submit to?"

20. You role play and rehearse.

This sounds like:

"Okay, Jack, so you're going to have your first interaction with a literary agent. What do you think about us role playing that a bit?"

Or:

"Okay, Mary, you say that you're ready to tell your father to stop bad mouthing your choice to write. Do you want to rehearse what you want to say to him?"

21. You express your worries and concerns.

This sounds like:

"You know, Jack, I'm a little worried that you won't be able to keep to your writing schedule while you're traveling. Can we think that through and see if we can come up with some tactics for writing while you travel?"

Or:

"Mary, I'm a little worried about you suggesting to your in-laws that they stay another month. Can we look at how that might play out around the writing?"

22. You refer.

This sounds like:

"Okay, Jack, if you intend to self-publish, you'll need someone to design the cover and someone to format the manuscript. If you go to the following website, you'll find a lot of recommendations for formatters and cover designers."

Or:

"Okay, Mary, it sounds like we're in a territory that I know very little about. Who do you think might be the right sort of person to help you with this?"

23. You invite new plans and new efforts.

This sounds like:

"Okay, Jack, we've tried a few things to get your morning writing practice in place, and it hasn't quite taken hold yet. What do you think we should try next?"

Or:

"Mary, it looks like you won't meet your goal of finishing your book by the summer unless we get some new strategies in place and unless we come up with a new plan. What are your thoughts on what a new plan might look like?"

24. You provide summaries and a sense of completion.

This sounds like:

"Okay, Jack, this session we've talked about getting a morning writing practice in place, replacing some habits that aren't serving you with some more useful ones and setting a daily word count goal. That's a lot! Congrats on all that!"

Or:

"Okay, Mary, for the past two months, you've been working to fit your writing into your real life, and you've managed to get an awful lot done! Congrats on that! How should we envision our work for the next month?"

Coaching really isn't fancier than this or different from this. You engage in common sense tactics that you believe will help your client identify and achieve her goals.

How Do You Respond?

Let's say that you're doing some existential coaching, which is an interesting coaching specialty, and a client presents you with a meaning-related issue. Consider the following presenting issue and five possible responses that a coach might make.

Your client says: "I don't know whether it makes more sense to reinvest meaning in my writing, even though I've never been able to get anything published, or to invest new meaning in photography, which I think interests me a lot."

One possible coach response is: "Tell me a little bit more about your history with writing. What have you written? What efforts have you made to get published? Tell me a bit about all that."

A second possible coach response is: "You say that photography interests you. I wonder, how do you usually go about distinguishing between mere interest and maybe deeper or more passionate interest?"

A third possible coach response is: "What if you were to try the following. What if you chose to write during the week and immerse yourself in photography on the weekends? How do you think that might work?"

A fourth possible coach response is: "What small action do you think you might want to take over the coming week to help you decide?"

A fifth possible coach response is: "You know, at the root of what you're experiencing may be the anxiety of choosing. I wonder if we could focus a little bit on anxiety."

Let's give a name to each of these five characteristic coach responses.

1. The first we might call an information draw, that is, the act of gathering a bit more information. That sounded like: "Tell me a little bit more about your history with writing. What have you written? What efforts have you made to get published? Tell me a bit about all that."

2. The second we might call a clarifying question, with perhaps a bit of educating built into the question. That sounded like: "You say that photography interests you. I wonder, how do you usually go about distinguishing between mere interest and deeper interest?"

3. The third we might call a problem-solving suggestion, with maybe a little educating thrown in. That sounded like: "What if you were to try the following? What if you chose to write during the week and immerse yourself in photography on the weekends? How do you think that might work?"

4. The fourth we might name a call to action, in the belief that almost any action is better than passivity. That sounded like: "What small action do you think you might want to take over the coming week to help you decide?"

5. The fifth we might call taking a useful tangent, that is, bringing up an idea of your own because you think it is useful or even crucial. That sounded like: "You know, at the root of what you're experiencing may be the anxiety of choosing. I wonder if we could focus a little bit on anxiety."

Here, then, are the five basic responses: information draw, clarifying question, problem-solving suggestion, call to action, and taking a useful tangent. Try your hand at thinking about this. A new client comes to you and says that he's an unhappy architect and wants to be coached on moving from architecture to something more fulfilling. How might you draw out some more information? What sort of clarifying question might you ask? What sort of problem-solving suggestion might you make? What would that sound like? What sort of call to action might you provide? What potentially useful tangent might you take? Take a moment and give this some thought!

The Coaching Session

How might a session with a client start? Here are eight common approaches, and all are perfectly sound.

1. "Hi, Gloria, why don't you catch me up a bit on what's been going on these past two weeks?"
2. "Hi, Gloria. Where would you like to start today?"
3. "Hi, Gloria. I thought we might start with what you wrote me last week about X. How did that play itself out?"
4. "Hi, Gloria. I think we ended our last chat focusing on X, and you were going to try Y. How did trying Y work out?
5. "Hi, Gloria. I was wondering how that problem with X was going? What's been up with that?"
6. "Hi, Gloria. I was thinking about what we talked about last time, and I had a question or two. Can we start with the questions that are on my mind?"
7. "Hi, Gloria. I can't wait to hear about X! Is that a good place to start?"
8. "Hi, Gloria. We've been focusing on X, Y, and Z. Want to catch me up on all three?"

In whatever way the session begins, the coach's goal is to get working. There may be an initial moment of pleasant chitchat, but both client and coach understand that this session is precious time devoted to helping the client with his issues. The coach aims her client in this direction by using prompts such as, "Catch me up a little on what we discussed last week," "Let's start with you filling me in on how approaching gallery owners went," or "I think you were going to work last week both on organizing your nonfiction book and rewriting the first part of your novel—which do you want to start with?" The coach focuses her client quickly on the serious matters at hand without wasting time or flinching.

Each session proceeds in its own way according to what the client presents. In one session, the client may be frustrated with himself and disappointed in his efforts, and the work of the session may be helping the client forgive himself and recommit to the same goals he 'failed at' the previous week. In another session, the client may have made a lot of progress and may not know what to tackle next, in which case the work is carefully and sensibly choosing the next goals. In another session, the client may want to meander and chitchat so as to avoid admitting that he hasn't done the work he said he would do, in which case the coach allows for a certain amount of meandering and chitchatting but sooner rather than later directly asks about the work, fully expecting to be presented with a sheepish confession.

This is a human interaction. Sometimes the coach listens; sometimes the coach coaxes; sometimes the coach teaches. In whatever way the coach operates, she dignifies the session with her humanness. She may have been trained to use a certain method, or she may have come to the conclusion that she will adopt a certain method, but in the end, she uses everything she possesses in order to be of help because no method really suffices. When she realizes that a coaching session is not so much about looking professional but rather about being of real service, she can relax into the fascinating work of being with another human being who is trying to make some progress.

Sessions take twists and turns. It isn't that you do a certain thing for 5 minutes, another thing for 10 minutes, and so on, but rather that, as in any conversation, you go back and forth and around and around in an effort to make sense of the issues at hand. You may start out a session checking in on how well your client managed to get to his screenplay and soon discover that you are discussing his desire to change careers, his longing to again play in a band, or the fact that his neighbors are making his life miserable. A person's reality is made up of disparate elements like these, and so is a coaching session.

Sometimes the two of you may get a little lost. What to do? Here are five things you might try:

1. "You know, Bob, I have the feeling that we should stop for a second and refocus. What do you think are the two or three things we ought to be focusing on?"

2.   "You know, Bob, I was just remembering from the first email you sent me that you wanted to work on X, Y, and Z. Are we paying good enough attention to those issues?"

3.   "You know, Bob, I wonder if maybe you could articulate one or two things you want to get accomplished in the coming two weeks. I think it would help me to hear what you have in mind."

4.   "You know, Bob, we have a new month starting in a few days, and maybe that's a great opportunity for us to refocus and recommit. What do you think you'd like to focus on in the new month?"

5.   "You know, Bob, I've been meaning to ask you about X. I don't think we've touched on X in a long time. Does it seem worth our time to pay a little attention to that?"

Thus, the coaching session proceeds. Probably a lot will get done! As you near the end of the session, you will want to 'begin to finish up' in the ways you have learned to finish up, perhaps by summarizing some key points. Coming to a sense of completion at the end of a session is a useful goal, and you want to avoid as much as possible ending a session with a sense that there's some unfinished business remaining. The trick is becoming very aware that only a few minutes remain and to learn how to effectively wind down a session so that it ends well.

Naturally, you also want to steer your client to the work he or she is to do between sessions. What exactly are you asking your client to do between sessions? You might be asking your client to do any of the following:

1.   You might ask him to work on whatever it is the two of you decided that he would work on. For example, in session, he might have mentioned that he felt ready to approach literary agents in the coming week. You agreed that was a great idea, and the two of you discussed what he needed to do in order to effectively approach agents, maybe focusing on him strengthening the subject line of his query email and the body of his query email. Therefore, at the end of the session you might say, "So, let me go over what we agreed on. In the coming week, you'll work on creating an effective subject line for your query email, strengthening the body of your email, and figuring out which agents you intend to approach. Does that sound right?"

2.   You might ask him to keep in touch with you about the progress he's making—or that he's not making. This might sound, "Okay, Frank, I know that you're going to try working on your first symphony this week. Please drop me an email when you get a chance and let me know

how that's going—including any obstacles that may have come up. Okay?" Even if your client isn't officially paying for email coaching, you might still sometimes make this offer of an email check-in.

3.   You might make this check-in even more formal by asking him to check in with you on a daily basis. This might sound like, "Okay, here's what I'd like you to do, if you feel like it might serve you. Every day after you've finished your two hours in the studio, just drop me a quick email that reads 'Done!' I may not respond to your email, or I may just say 'Congrats!' What do you think about checking in daily?" If your client feels that checking in that way serves him, then that becomes part of his work between sessions.

4.   You might ask her to report on a particular event or interaction. This might sound like, "Okay, Mary, that editor said that she'd be in touch with you this week, and we've rehearsed how you want to respond to the questions she's likely to ask you. Do you want to check in after you've spoken with her and let me know how it went? I'd love to hear! What are your thoughts on checking in with me via email after you've chatted with her?"

The session ends—but your client's work doesn't end. Part of your helpfulness as a coach is pressing your client to work between sessions on her goals, her dreams, and her aspirations.

Following, Leading, Interrupting, and Inviting

During a given session, you might do all of the following:

- You might listen as your client tries to articulate his issues.
- You might ask questions to help you better understand what your client is getting at.
- You might help your client arrive at concrete goals.
- You might cheerlead and help motivate your client.
- You might single out something your client said because you consider it important.
- You might make suggestions and problem solve.
- You might teach a little.
- You might come to an agreement about what your client will work on between sessions.

As a coach, you are both following and leading. Sometimes you will follow your client, and sometimes you will lead your client. A client may frame a problem in a certain way and, although you want to support her way of framing the problem, at the same time, you may believe that she is making a conscious or an unconscious mistake. She may believe, for example, that she is supposed to wait for inspiration before she begins her new career, an idea you might accept if she hadn't been waiting for this particular inspiration for three years already. You have the feeling that something very different is going on—maybe that she is too sad to begin, maybe that she doesn't believe that there are sufficient reasons to start this career, maybe she is struggling too hard just to survive, and so on—and that 'waiting for inspiration' is a way of avoiding looking too closely at what is really going on in her life.

How will you proceed? By remembering that you have permission to lead and by remembering not to be frightened of being real, just as long as you are gentle while being real. This might sound in your own head like the following:

> I have no investment as to whether she will or won't begin this new career. In fact, I have my doubts that she will begin it, and I don't want to get too attached to needing her to begin. But I would like to understand why she is having so much trouble beginning, and I would like to support her desire to begin. So, I think that I'll ask her what's getting in the way of her starting, in addition to not feeling inspired. Maybe that will provide us both with some clues as to how we might proceed. Although I doubt that her formulation about what is preventing her from starting her new career is on target, I will honor her formulation of the issue but also check in about what *else* she thinks may be going on here.

By checking in with her about what may be preventing her from starting her new career "along with not feeling inspired," you are subtly arguing that something else is probably going on. But you are not flatly disputing her formulation of the situation. By being careful and circumspect, you are likely to allow her to drop her defenses and to think more clearly and genuinely about the situation. You are leading but not in a high-handed or aggressive manner. The subtleties of these dynamics can only be learned by monitoring how clients react to the responses you make and by noticing what helps and what doesn't help.

If you are a problem-solving sort of person, you may find it hard to follow and to accept your client's version of the situation. On the other hand, if you do not have much experience in leading others or if leading isn't your current style, you may find it hard to aim a person in a direction of your choosing.

Whichever is more difficult for you, following or leading, work on that skill by leading more if you find it hard to lead and by following more if you find it hard to follow. Ultimately, both skills are required.

You'll also want to learn how to strategically interrupt. If you let your clients tell their stories without interruption—because you find the flow useful, out of politeness, because you're not sure when to interrupt, and so on—then you will need to present your stored-up inquiries when your client has finished telling his story. This can prove really hard if your client has gone on for a bit and there are now several things on your mind. Therefore, regularly interrupting may be the better bet, especially if you've learned how to return a client to his narrative thread.

You can interrupt, ask a question, take in the information you receive, and return your client to his story by apologizing, "Before I interrupted, you were saying—" I think that this sort of "useful interrupting" is worth incorporating into whatever style of coaching you choose.

The following are among the sorts of useful interruptions I have in mind.

Your client says, "I've always wanted to compose, but I don't have anything musically to say—."

You might immediately interrupt and say, "I'd like to check in on that. What exactly do you mean by, 'You don't have anything musically to say'? I'm worried that speaking to yourself like that may be part of the problem!"

Maybe your client says, "I have several paintings that are done, maybe enough for a show—"

You might interrupt and ask, "Do you mean that you do have enough paintings for a show or that you don't quite have enough paintings for a show? It wasn't so clear to me which you were meaning."

Your client might reply, "Oh, I have enough paintings for a show, but I can't afford the framing, and I don't have good slides—"

Then you can say, "Oh, I see! That's much clearer. We'll certainly get back to this. I think you were saying before I interrupted you that you have several paintings done, maybe enough for a show—"

Sometimes you might interrupt, listen to your client's response, and then pursue what your client has just brought up rather than allowing him to return to his narrative thread. This might sound like the following:

Your client: "I couldn't just call a literary agent cold."

You, interrupting: "Still, is that a stretch you'd like to make?"

Your client: "No. It's too scary!"

You, now pursuing this thread: "But what if you were sufficiently prepared?"

Your client: "Prepared, how?"

You: "Let's talk about that. How does a person get ready to talk to a literary agent?"

Or:

Your client: "I just don't think I can speak other people's lines one more time! It's just too boring! I can't make myself audition—"

Your strategic interruption: "What about speaking your own lines? Is it maybe the time to write a performance piece?"

Your client: "I've been thinking about that for the longest time."

You: "And?"

Your client: "I don't know. Those are different skills. I'm not sure I'm talented in that way—"

You: "But you do want to write a performance piece? Do you want to speak in your own voice?"

Your client: "I do."

You: "Okay, then! Let's focus on that for a few minutes."

Sometimes you interrupt because you need clarification or more information. Sometimes you interrupt because you want to take the lead and steer your client in a certain direction. Sometimes you interrupt because you want to educate or consult. The basic rhythm of a session, whether conducted in person or on the phone, is for a client to present her thoughts and for you to ask questions and sometimes to interrupt your client's answers with further questions.

If it isn't in your nature to interrupt or if it isn't a habit with you to interrupt, you may find yourself confronted by long narratives that contain so much unaddressed material that you have no idea where to begin or what to say when your client has finished speaking. It is a much better policy to interrupt a long narrative with intentional questions that allow you to coach as you go. In the sense in which I've just described, interrupting is an important habit to acquire.

Then there's the tactic of 'offering invitations.' Whatever style you develop, the technique of 'offering invitations' is a useful technique to fold into your personal style. In addition to whatever else you do as you coach, you can always offer your client a certain sort of invitation. For example, you might invite her to try her hand at some things she might enjoy attempting that, for one reason or another, she is not currently pursuing.

Let's say that your client might well love to submit her latest short story to a well-known magazine but doesn't have the courage to try. You might invite her to try. She might relish studying a new painting technique but not have thought to learn something new. You might invite her to try. She might profit from turning her research into a nonfiction book but not know how to begin.

You might invite her to try. You can invite her to attempt things that she has told you she would like to try, and you can also invite her to try things that you independently think she might benefit from doing.

The following are some examples of invitations that you might offer to a writer client:

1. "Mary, I noticed that this month's *Writer's Digest* is devoted to writers' conferences. Since we talked about you possibly attending one, I thought I'd let you know. Care to take a look at the issue and report back?"
2. "Mary, I was watching the Weather Channel and noticed that you're starting to get some warm weather. Since we talked about you writing outdoors this spring, I wondered if you were giving that any thought?"
3. "Mary, you mentioned in passing that you had put aside a half-completed nonfiction book last year. I wonder if you'd like to talk about that. Should we bring that to a front burner?"
4. "Mary, I just remembered that you have a meeting coming up with a literary agent! I wonder if you'd like to role play and rehearse that meeting?"
5. "Mary, I just happened upon some inexpensive Internet writing courses that looked interesting. Would you like the link?"
6. "Mary, you say that you have a lot more research to do before you can start on your article. Yet you sound extremely well informed about your subject. I wonder if you could write a draft right now using what you currently know?"
7. "Mary, I know that your publisher is looking for another romance, but I wonder if it's time to take a break from writing what no longer interests you and try your hand at the adventure novel we've been talking about?"
8. "Mary, I think you may be stymied in writing your historical novel by not being able to really picture 11th-century Madrid. Would you like to spend a couple of weeks doing some research?"
9. "Mary, I just read an interview with a literary agent who claims to love representing exactly the kind of book you're writing. I know that contacting agents has seemed scary to you, but I wonder if you might like to contact this one?"
10. "Mary, I think you mentioned that you wanted to try a novel after you wrote your short stories. Now that the story collection is done, is it time to think about that novel?"

If you have an empathic understanding of your client's situation and inner landscape, you will naturally want to invite her to try out things that you know are already on her mind or that are just out of her conscious awareness and that she would love to try if only someone mentioned them to her. There is virtually no risk in extending these invitations and a tremendous upside because your client may be thrilled to receive your one- or two-sentence invitation and may even be transformed by it.

Your Coaching Style

Naturally, you are going to want to coach your way, in a style that makes sense to you and that suits your personality. Each coach brings his or her own style to the table, and for most coaches, that styles evolves over time, often moving from a so-to-speak aggressive problem-solving style—let's get your problems fixed!—to a more measured, collaborative approach that includes a lot of listening.

Here are eight characteristic coaching styles: the listener, the problem solver, the teacher, the expert, the taskmaster, the peer, the friend, and the cheerleader. Let's imagine how a coach might speak to his client, Jane, who is trying to start an Internet business.

Here's how 'the listener' might sound:

"Jane, I think that you're saying that you can't find the motivation to start your Internet business. Can you tell me a little bit more about why it's feeling so hard to get motivated?"

Here's how 'the problem solver' might sound:

"Okay, Jane, you say that the first step in setting up your Internet business is deciding about your website. Why don't you do a search and see if you can find half a dozen websites that you think work well and write down what exactly about them seems to be working."

Here's how 'the teacher' might sound:

"Okay, Jane, starting an Internet business always has a lot of moving parts, and the key is getting organized and staying organized. What sort of organizational scheme do you want to put into place so that you stay organized?"

Here's how 'the expert' might sound:

"You know, Jane, the key to any successful Internet business is branding. That's the number one key to success. So, tell me a little bit about what's unique about your brand."

Here's how 'the taskmaster' might sound:

"Okay, Jane, you said that you'd be able to spend three hours a day on your Internet business, but that only happened on one or two days last week. Let's learn from what happened last week and let's set some new goals for this coming week, shall we?"

Here's how 'the peer' might sound:

"Jane, when I started my first Internet business, I found it especially hard to figure out what my website ought to look like and how it ought to function. Are you having those same difficulties?"

Here's how 'the friend' might sound:

"Wow, Jane, what a hard few days you've had! That must have been terrible, hearing that news about your mother. No wonder you haven't gotten anything done on your Internet business!"

Here's how 'the cheerleader' might sound:

"Jane, that's excellent news that you got in 10 full hours this week on building your business! Keep up the good work! That's really great!"

Naturally, your style will evolve over time. Each of us has a predominant style nearer one end or the other end of the directive–nondirective continuum. A very directive person is typically in a hurry to problem solve. A very nondirective person is reluctant to offer suggestions, teach, or try out assignments. An effective coach combines elements of directive and nondirective coaching, being brave enough to risk making suggestions and ego-less enough to just listen. You may want to keep track of your evolving style by monitoring the emails you send to your clients and thinking through what your responses say about the style you're cultivating.

Your Five Goals as A Coach

Your first goal is trying to be of help. There are countless strategies and tactics you can use to be of help. You can make suggestions, offer opinions, explain what has worked and what hasn't worked for you, provide exercises and homework, focus on some area that you think is particularly important, and so on. The main point to keep in mind is the simple sounding but profound idea that you mean to be of help.

Your second goal is to not attach to outcomes. You want to detach from outcomes and expectations, making sure not to get invested in your client's dramas. You want to provide your client with the genuine freedom to go where he or she needs to go. This is not the same thing as having no stake in the process. The stake you have is your obligation to be present and to try your best to be of help. But you cannot make another person do anything— write her novel, create meaning, get ahead at work, and so on. Only she can do those things. You cannot have as *your* goal that she completes her novel or make a job change; only she can have such goals.

Your third goal is to try to understand. If we're listening well, we understand when a person is sounding afraid, down on herself, overwhelmed by current circumstances, unmotivated, and so on. We also understand what to suggest in such circumstances, if we think about it. We can suggest a small thing to try, a belief or behavior to begin to change, and so on. If you really don't know how to think about the situation, then you ask your client to tell you more. As she tells you more, answers may come to her or they may come to you. This is the process of understanding.

Your fourth goal is to show support and to actually *feel* supportive. This might sound like "That sounds hard!" or "That was excellent work you did this week!" What can get in the way of you supporting another person? It might be that you're too adamant about the 'right way' things should be done. It might be your inability to get out of your own shoes and see the world through another person's eyes. It might be your bitterness about not having been supported enough yourself. When you don't feel supportive, that may mean that your client is being pointedly difficult, or it may mean that some shadowy thing has cropped up in you. Your main personal work as a coach may be to so-to-speak 'soften' into a genuinely supportive person.

Your fifth goal is to be real. When you are pretty certain that your client is misinformed about something or has misconstrued something, you want to have internal permission to tell her what's on your mind. You will need to say this very carefully, as any difference of opinion can—and usually does—feel like criticism. But if, for example, she believes that she can find a literary agent to handle her poetry, when literary agents do not handle poetry, you will want to find the way to reality test and speak the truth. This is also the area where you bring in accountability. Being real means reminding clients that they agreed to do this or that, and so you make it your business to check in on your client's efforts in a noncritical, supportive, but firm way.

If you decide to coach creative and performing artists, you would then have a sixth goal: to understand their particular issues and to develop strategies for helping that particular population. You'll have noticed that, in the case studies presented in this book, all of the following issues surfaced: sadness; anxiety; frustration; disappointments; uncertainty about what to create, why to create, and how to create; difficulties in getting to the work, doing the work, and selling the work; painful existential questions about meaning; resistance to planning, scheduling, and concrete goal setting; and countless practical and emotional challenges, from chronic illness to chronic poverty to caregiving duties to personality shortfalls. Clients with these issues await you!

Appendix

II

Supplemental Reading

Barry, Lynda. *Syllabus: Notes from an Accidental Professor*. Montreal, Canada: Drawn and Quarterly (October 21, 2014)

Cameron, Julia. *The Artist's Way: 25th Anniversary Edition*. New York, NY: Tarcher/Perigee (October 25, 2016)

Currey, Mason. *Daily Rituals: How Artists Work*. New York, NY: Knopf (April 23, 2013)

Gilbert, Elizabeth. *Big Magic: Creative Living Beyond Fear*. New York, NY: Riverhead Books (September 27, 2016)

Kimsey-House, Karen and Henry Kimsey-House. *Co-Active Coaching, Fourth Edition*. Boston, MA: Nicholas Brealey (July 10, 2018)

Kleon, Austin. *Steal Like an Artist: 10 Things Nobody Told You About Being Creative*. New York, NY: Workman Publishing (February 28, 2012)

Maisel, Eric. *Become a Creativity Coach Now!* Walnut Creek, CA: Crossways Press (February 12, 2018)

Maisel, Eric. *Coaching the Artist Within*. Novato, CA: New World Library (September 24, 2010)

Maisel, Eric. *Creative Recovery*. Boulder, CO: Shambhala (October 14, 2008)

Maisel, Eric. *Fearless Creating*. New York, NY: Tarcher/Perigee (October 17, 1995)

Maisel, Eric. *Mastering Creative Anxiety*. Novato, CA: New World Library (March 9, 2011)

Maisel, Eric. *Secrets of a Creativity Coach*. Carlsbad, CA: Motivational Press (December 5, 2013)

Maisel, Eric. *Unleashing the Artist Within*. Mineola, NY: Dover (April, 2020)

Maisel, Eric. *The Van Gogh Blues*. Novato, CA: New World Library (August 21, 2012)

Martin, Curly. *The Life Coaching Handbook*. Bancyfelin, UK: Crown House Pub Ltd (March 1, 2002)

Menendez, Diane and Patrick Williams. *Becoming a Professional Life Coach: Lessons from the Institute of Life Coach Training*. New York, NY: W. W. Norton & Company (March 23, 2015)

Stanier, Michael Bungay. *The Coaching Habit: Say Less, Ask More & Change the Way You Lead Forever*. Toronto, Canada: Box of Crayons Press (February 29, 2016)

Stoltzfus, Tony. *Coaching Questions: A Coach's Guide to Powerful Asking Skills*. Southborough, MA: Coach22 Bookstore LLC (April 24, 2008)

Tharp, Twyla. *The Creative Habit: Learn It and Use It for Life*. New York, NY: Simon & Schuster (January 6, 2006)

Wilson, Megan Jo. *Who The F*ck Am I to Be a Coach?! A Warrior's Guide to Building a Wildly Successful Coaching Business from the Inside out*. Chicago, IL: Becoming Journey LLC (March 13, 2018)

Index

10 Delightful Ways Travel Can Change Your Life 34

A.B.C.D.E. model of cognitive psychology 143–144
Allan, E. V. 15
Aniballi, F. 175
Arbach, N. 127–128
Art for Well-Being program 46
artists: dreams coming true for 36–39; marketing themselves 141–144; returning to the marketplace 51–53; self-taught 11–14
Artist's Way, The 77, 91, 92

Badonsky, J. 70
Barrio, B. M. 99
Become a Creativity Coach Now 176
Bixler, L. 185
Block-Buster 10
blocked creativity coaches 41–44
blocked writers 26–29
Bosshard, A. 155
Bourne, H. 75
breathing exercises 23
Burton, S. J. 80

Cameron, J. 77, 91, 92
centering 24
Chaudhry, P. 136
Christie, S. 85
clearing physical and mental clutter to unleash creativity 123–126
coaching: coaches' goals in 213–214; defining 196–197; following, leading, interrupting, and inviting in 207–212; individuals styles of 212–213; nuts and bolts of tactics in 198–202; possible responses in 203–204; structure of sessions in 204–207
Cohen, S. 109
competing demands, managing 137–139
confidence: breeding creativity 71–73; in career building for designers 110–113; *see also* self-doubt
creativity: clearing physical and mental clutter to unleash 123–126; confidence breeding 71–73; facing obligations while committing to 161–164; fear of 95–98; financial outcomes of 105–108; finding voice and flow in 166–169; group coaching for 90–92; imposter syndrome and 76–79; inspired by travel 31–34; liminal spaces and 181–184; and managing overwhelm and inefficiency 137–139; navigating the maze of 176–179; restoring 100–103; self-sabotaging of 171–174; small, simple, and every day 81–84; sparked by foundation of health and well-being 156–159; stopping naysaying to fulfill potential in 146–148; through leadership 186–188; time-limited creative exercises for 115–117

Dadamio, N. 104
de Búrca, R. 165
designers: career steps for 110–113; risk and detachment as key skills for 1–4
divorce 61–64
dreams coming true 36–39

Edwards, G. 20
enneagram 119–122
entrepreneurship 32–33
expectations, lowered 66–69

fear of art-making 95–98
fibromyalgia 56–59
filmmakers 46–49
financial success 105–108

Garratt, S. 55
Good, S. 40
Gorfien, R. 60
Grace, A. 5
group creativity coaching 90–92

health: divorce and 61–64; fibromyalgia and
    56–59; and overall well-being, returning
    to 46–49; sparking new creative energy
    through 156–159
Holder, J. 170

imposter syndrome 76–79

Johnston, J. 122
Johnston, N. 118
Joseph, V. 140
journaling, finding voice and flow through
    166–169

Kelvin, T. 189
Koulouri, N. A. 145

Langer, E. 7
Lazaris, N. 25
leadership, creativity through 186–188
liminal spaces and creativity 181–184
limiting beliefs 143–144

Maguire, J. 195
Maisel, E. 176, 190
marketing by artists 141–144
Marsden, R. 45
Mazák, S. 114
mental rehearsal, positive 23–24
midlife, travel and creativity in 31–34
Moore, J. 35
muscle relaxation 24
*Muse Is In: An Owner's Manual to Your
    Creativity, The* 70
musicians: stage fright in 21–24; transitioning
    from day jobs to full-time 133–135

navigating the maze of creativity 176–179
nutrition and health 47–48

On Becoming an Artist 7
Overcome Stage Fright Forever 25
overwhelm and inefficiency 137–139

pain: art linked to suffering and 95–98; of
    divorce 61–64; fibromyalgia 56–59
painters: restoring vibrancy to life 100–103;
    self-taught 11–14
Penley, M. 30
perfectionism 66–69
performance anxiety 21–24
Phoenix, R. 65
photographers 56–59
podcasting 76, 80
Pomodoro technique 42
Poreba, D. M. 94
positive mental rehearsal 23–24
positive self-talk 23, 77
Post-Divorce Bliss: Ending Us and Finding Me 89
private tutoring 129–131

Raine, D. 160
rewriting from scratch 151–154
Rieger, S. 132
risk and detachment skills 1–4

self-doubt 71–73, 81–84, 146–148; limiting
    beliefs and 143–144; *see also* confidence
self-sabotaging 171–174
self-talk, positive 23, 77
self-taught painters 11–14
sewists 123–126
Soteriou, N. 50
Spark Your Creative podcast 80
stage fright 21–24
starting over in writing 151–154
storytellers, visual 171–174
subpersonality work for blocked writers
    26–29
Sylvester, L. B. 180

Terris, A. 150
Thorbes, C. 10
time-limited creative exercises 115–117
timid creatives 6–9
transitioning from a day job to music career
    133–135
Trauma-Informed Expressive Arts Therapy
    136
travel and creativity 31–34
tutoring, private 129–131

values aligned with creative work
    16–19
vibrancy, restoring 100–103

visual storytellers 171–174
voice and flow, finding one's 166–169

Walsh, J. 89
well-being *see* health
Work on Your Own Terms in Midlife & Beyond 35
writers: aligning values with their work 16–19; blocked 26–29, 41–44; committing to creative work while facing obligations 161–164; constructing a creative life 81–84; finding voice and flow through journaling and writing 166–169; hundred consecutive days of writing practice for 86–87; perfectionism in 66–69; returning to the marketplace 51–53; rewriting from scratch 151–154; self-doubt in 71–73; timid 6–9; working to finish projects using goals and deadlines 190–194

For Product Safety Concerns and Information please contact our EU
representative GPSR@taylorandfrancis.com
Taylor & Francis Verlag GmbH, Kaufingerstraße 24, 80331 München, Germany